ENDORSEMENTS

I have known Richard Meza for over 40 years now and I can truthfully say our friendship has been a special one. If I recall correctly, he is my junior by four years (he never lets me forget it). From the time we met in the early 70s, I have been astounded by his childlike faith. He has always ventured into challenging situations without fear, so much so that you could categorize him as "reckless" in his approach to spiritual situations. I say that in a good way because time after time observing him fight against the enemy, it was the only way that Satan could be defeated. I realize now after so many years, it was God's way of preparing him for even greater challenges he would have to endure not only in his personal life but also his family whom he loves more than anything else.

I know that all of us suffer at one time or another; I also am cognizant of the fact that God calls certain people to endure suffering as an entry way to experience the glory of God like few of His children. Richard and Tabitha (his wife) are two such people. The attacks on their lives have come in droves and in all directions, at times with great, heart wrenching intensity. No one in the family has been exempt and it is mind-boggling that anyone in the Meza family continues to serve God. That being said, I understand now after observing for many years that this "trial by fire" has been the steppingstone that makes them shine like gold.

The testimonies and or lessons Richard will share have not come from a book or from someone else's experiences. Everything you read is not only first-hand, but it also has not been manufactured to move your emotions. The suffering endured is real and we can only conclude that God is true to His word for anyone who will allow Him to move miraculously in their lives. If you will take the time to read these blogs with an open heart, your life will truly be blessed. The knowledge, encouragement, and wisdom you gain will not only uplift your soul, but they will also draw you closer to God. ENJOY!

George Pantages
Evangelist/Author

In every generation, God uniquely calls men and women to represent HIS heart, in character, in conversation, and in conduct, and Pastor Richard Meza is the genuine article or "real thing"—this being the essence of what true "servant leadership" is all about. As the role of a pastor has dramatically changed during the past four decades, in becoming even more increasingly challenging and demanding for even the most devoted at heart; statistically, close to 1,500 pastors close down their churches every month, due to both the rabid demands and the lack of human and financial support needed to build their churches according to God's Will. In Pastor Meza's book, *Building Up The Temple: The Little Church That Could*, he provides the practical guidance and powerful insights that any young minister or pastor would need to grow into the simple steps of faith required "to see God build HIS church", and do the impossible no matter how large or small the congregation. I recommend this book for any sincere Christian leader that wants to avoid the known pitfalls, possess the wisdom of God for the building process, and be prayerfully positioned for whatever God will do in the life of HIS church or local fellowship.

Pastor Walter L. Smith III, Founder/President of The Center For Kingdom Advancement/Pure In Heart Int'l Ministries, Inc.

BUILDING UP
THE TEMPLE

BUILDING UP
THE TEMPLE

The Little Church That Could

Richard Meza

Library of Congress Control Number:		2015915253
ISBN:	Hardcover	978-1-5144-0820-9
	Softcover	978-1-5144-0821-6
	eBook	978-1-5144-0822-3

Print information available on the last page.

Rev. date: 09/18/2015

To order additional copies of this book, contact:
Xlibris
1-888-795-4274
www.Xlibris.com
Orders@Xlibris.com
708683

CONTENTS

F IRST AND FOREMOST, I would like to dedicate this book to my Lord and Savior, Jesus Christ. I think it goes without saying that this beautiful sanctuary was built first and foremost by the mighty hand of God.

I would also like to dedicate this book to my wonderful wife, Tabitha, who has been a shining example of Christian integrity and faithfulness for all her life. Even after years of battling so many health issues—three brain tumor operations, four strokes, TMJ operations, years of epilepsy, being in a wheelchair three times, and other sicknesses—she remains constant in her love and commitment to God and her family. She has been my constant advisor and my kindred spirit throughout the years, and I am so proud to be her husband. She, along with my children, has been the true hero during the building of the sanctuary. I would also like to thank my children, Ashly Elizabeth, Richie, and Isaiah, for all that they have endured during those early years. I have been blessed by the Lord to have such an awesome family.

I would also like to thank my brother-in-law, Pastor Prospero Jacobo, and his wife, First Lady Esther Jacobo, who came to help us at the right time and never left us alone. I would also like to thank my in-laws (both of whom are now with the Lord), Pastor Silvestre and Eva Pena, who fully supported us in this endeavor. I also want to thank the many individuals and businesses that helped us during the construction of the sanctuary. I would also like to thank all the unofficial church historians, like Sister Carmen Robles, Carmen Madrigal, Sister Angie Leal, Sister Isabel Butanda, Sister Olga Topete, and of course, Sister Eva Salinas, but most of all, I want to thank Sister Blanca Gallardo for her tireless effort in helping secure everything, from old members' names to taking pictures needed to complete this book. It goes without saying that I also want to thank Mr. Thurman Alexander, who has also gone to be with the Lord, who dedicated his life, equipment, experience, expertise, and monies toward the success of this project.

I would also like to thank the congregation of Mendota Apostolic Church, who, despite my youth and inexperience, backed me up 100 percent and dared to believe God would grant them their miracle. This wonderful and spunky congregation will definitely qualify to be included as heroes of faith, as described in the book of Hebrews.

Last of all, I would like to dedicate this book to every young and inexperienced pastor who has been told "You can't do it," "You'll never do it," or "It isn't ever going to happen!" While experience is definitely a plus, God will use you, if you are willing, to be a vessel for His honor and glory. I have made every effort to present an unvarnished and true life account of what God has done and can do even if you don't qualify to be counted as a spiritual giant.

CHAPTER 1

The Beginning:
God Sends a Messenger

IT ALL BEGAN one sunny weekend in 1986, while we were living in the beautiful city of Escondido, California. Escondido is a picturesque city approximately thirty-five miles north of San Diego; it has all the amenities you will want in a place that you will want to settle down and raise a family in. This was the case for Tabitha and me; we had found the perfect place to start and raise our family in.

During those years, we had pretty much settled down into a stable and contented lifestyle. I worked as assistant pastor to Pastor Frank Villa at the Escondido Apostolic Church. Tabitha and I both felt very satisfied because we were working for the Lord in such areas as Sunday school, the youth department, the bus ministry, and some other ministries.

On the material side, we were also in pretty good shape. Since Tabitha and I were both employed, we had bought our first home, we owned three vehicles, and we even had some half-season tickets to both the San Diego Padres and the Chargers. We were also very fortunate because after seven years of waiting for children, we were blessed by God with a beautiful baby girl we named Ashly Elizabeth. In a nutshell, we had everything that we needed and wanted—we truly felt blessed by the Lord.

But this was not the case, because for a few months, something had been tugging at my heart. At first, I couldn't quite put my finger on it, but I did know that I felt almost like a sense of restlessness and dissatisfaction. I just did not feel happy. I felt that even though we seemed to have everything, something was missing. After feeling like this for a few months, I soon realized that God was just beginning to deal with us.

My cousin Gloria and her husband, George, had come down from Los Angeles to spend the weekend with us. We had always enjoyed their company as George and I had attended the same church in East Los Angeles when we were young converts in the Lord many years before. We so looked forward to our conversations of the USC Trojans football and the UCLA Bruins basketball teams, the Los Angeles Lakers, and of course, those famous Los Angeles Dodgers! But this visit turned out to be quite different. When I sat down with George and explained what I had been feeling, he cocked his head to one side (as was his habit) and told me what he felt in his heart. Because I really respected his opinion, I listened intently to what he had to say, because as far as I was concerned, if anyone knew about doing God's will, it would be George. He was one of the top prospects coming out of high school in the nation as a kicker and, in fact, was already signed up to play football for the USC Trojans. Yet when the Lord spoke to George and told him what He wanted from him, he gave it all up to give his life to the Lord and, eventually, to enter the ministry, where he is now an international evangelist who preaches all over the world.

As George began to relate to me what he felt from the Lord, I soon began to realize that God had sent a messenger to awaken Tabitha and me from our spiritual slumber. He told me about what it was to truly be in God's will and how one must forge a deep and meaningful relationship with God. At this point in my life, without realizing it, I had become a materialistic person. I had justified myself because of my many activities at church. The bottom line was that we had become like the church of Ephesus, as described in Revelations 2:2–4: "I know your works . . . your patience, and that you cannot bear those who are evil. And you have tested those who say they are apostles and are not, and have found them liars; and you have persevered and have patience, and have labored for My name's sake and have not become weary. Nevertheless I have *this* against you, that you have left your first love." I had forgotten how so many years before, at my age of fourteen, as I came out of the baptismal waters, God had put a burning desire in my heart to one day become a pastor. So as George talked to me, I began to understand that what I had been doing for the last few years was simply spinning my spiritual wheels.

RICHARD MEZA

The old church at 807 Quince Ave.

The new church at 636 Juanita Ave.

CHAPTER 2

The Move

AFTER HEARING WHAT God had to say to me by way of George, I realized that we had to make a move. Tabitha and I, after a time of prayer and consecration, started really seeking the will of God. We gave notices to our respective employers, put our home up for sale, and started to make preparations for our move. The only problem was that we had no idea where we were going!

We first considered moving to a small town called Patterson, which is located in central California. We had gone to visit one of Tabitha's friends who lives there and had fallen in love with Patterson. We also talked about other places we had visited, but in the end, we decided it was best to leave that decision to the will of God. It was about that time, after my father-in-law had gotten wind of what we were contemplating, that he and my mother-in-law decided to go visit. He confessed to us that he had been praying for us and that he was very pleased to hear that we were willing to spread our wings. He offered to help us, in any way possible, to reach our goal and, in fact, had already contacted Rev. Manuel Viscarra (a good friend of his), who, at that time, was the president of our organization. After my father-in-law contacted him, Reverend Viscarra requested that we come up to Riverside to meet with him. Things seemed to come together rather quickly once we had made our decision to be fully committed to make our move in accordance to God's will.

We drove down to see Reverend Viscarra at his church in Riverside, California, one Sunday afternoon. We got there just as the church service got started, so we went in and joined the service. We asked one of the ushers to please notify Reverend Viscarra that we had arrived. As we sat there in the service, I began to contemplate what was happening in our life. It occurred to me that whatever the outcome of this meeting, we should regard it as God's will, and above all, we needed to be obedient to His call. To say that we were nervous and worried would be an understatement, but one thing I learned that day was that once you took that first step of faith, God would give you the strength and direction that you would need to complete your journey. I don't mind telling you that by the time we were escorted to his office, I was a complete bundle of nerves. Reverend Viscarra asked us whether we had a game plan or not, to which we replied that we did not. After listening to us about our initial idea about Patterson, he explained to us that there were so many churches throughout the nation that were in need of a good pastor. I asked Reverend Viscarra if we could have a moment alone, then I told Tabitha what I felt in my heart, and she agreed with me, that we were going to put ourselves completely in the hands of God, and wherever it was that Reverend Viscarra felt God would send us, that was where we would be, ready and willing to go. After mentioning faraway places like San Antonio, Texas; Fairfield, California; and Pueblo, Colorado, he said he was going to wait and pray for God's direction and would get back to us shortly. I left the meeting with mixed emotions because along with the sense of apprehension and worry that I felt, I could not also help feeling a real sense of excitement. We really began to wonder where in the world the Lord would send us, but at least we knew one thing for sure in our hearts, that we were no longer spinning our spiritual wheels.

It seemed to take an eternity before, one evening, late at night, I finally got a call from Reverend Viscarra. Because I had been in a deep sleep when he called, right when our conversation ended, I thanked him, and without saying good-bye, I unceremoniously hung up on him. It was not until the next morning that I realized what I had done. I made a mental note to make sure to call Reverend Viscarra and apologize to him for having hung up on him. What he told me during our phone conversation was that the church we were going to pastor was in a little town called Mendota. I went straight to the garage and pulled out an old U-Haul atlas from 1977. I frantically searched for Mendota, but at first, I could not find it. After a while, when I found it, I saw that Mendota was a small town located just west of Fresno, California, smack between Interstate 5 and Highway 99 in the middle of nowhere. To my consternation, the population of Mendota, according to the atlas, was listed at just 3,777 people. I thought to myself, *Where in the world are you sending us to, Lord?* What was more was that when I mentioned Mendota to my friends, I was surprised that many of them had heard of it as being a small town where many of their relatives had gone to work in the fields. Nevertheless, we were resolved to go wherever the Lord wanted us to go, even if it was to this small town that was located in the middle of nowhere.

I found it quite peculiar that during the time we got ready to make our move, some strange things began to happen in our lives. First off, I began to have trouble at work when I notified them I was leaving; somehow, they seemed to feel that after all they had done for me, how could I leave them? Then we began to get bothered by an evil spirit that would constantly harass us, especially at night. I believe that it was Satan letting us know that he was ready to battle with us because of our decision. This continued night after night until one evening, when the situation finally came to a head. As I was on my knees, praying, in the living room, my infant daughter Ashly Elizabeth woke up crying. As I picked her up into my arms, I could feel that the evil presence was in her room and that it was frightening my baby. This made me feel very angry, and I felt such a spirit of indignation that this spirit not only dared to invade our home but also to bother my Ashly, so I called this spirit out and commanded it in the name of Jesus to leave our house. Almost immediately a great peace came into our house, and I knew that God had given us the victory. Another thing that happened during this time was that we began to feel a real sense of loss. As I had mentioned at the beginning, Tabitha and I had made the decision that we planned to live in Escondido for the rest of our lives. We had established our roots here for so many years, but now we were about to leave behind all our friends, family, hopes, ambitions, etc. It was truly a time of deep reflection and a time to really examine ourselves.

These are the times when you really learn that this is serious business and that you want to make sure you are in the perfect will of God. It's also a time when you see yourself beginning to go through a transformation of sorts, because you begin to have such a much deeper relationship with God. It also causes you to change from a spiritually insensitive, self-centered, self-justifying, materialistic state to a frame of mind where your only purpose is to want to please God and to do His will.

CHAPTER 2A

Mendota, USA

T HERE IS AN old adage that says "First impressions are lasting impressions." I can tell you from experience that this is not always the case.

It was on a Saturday morning that we arrived in Fresno and saw the exit sign that read Mendota: Highway 180 West. According to the directions we received, all we had to do was follow Highway 180, heading west, until it ended right at Mendota. After being on the road for a while, I noticed that the landscape started to change as we got farther from Fresno, especially as we started passing through small towns like Rolinda, Tranquillity, San Joaquin, and Kerman. After a while, all semblance of city life was gone and had now been replaced by an agricultural setting with cotton fields, lush green rolling fields, and beautiful trees. I will tell you the truth; at that moment, I really began to feel pretty good about where God was taking us.

But then as we neared our destination, all the lush green fields and pretty green trees all of a sudden began to disappear and were now replaced with barren fields with alkaline-like white sand and, every once in a while, short shrub-like trees. When I saw the worried look on Tabitha's face, I turned to her and tried to reassure her by telling her that I was sure God was taking us to a very beautiful place. Wouldn't you know, it was just about then that we were hit by a very bad smell that came from a Spreckels Sugar processing plant that was just up the road; only those of you who have been around such a plant can fully appreciate what I mean, because that acrid, stinky odor hits your sense of smell like a ton of bricks. Then as you turn into Mendota, there is also a trash-conversion plant that contributes even more to the smell.

After we had lived in a picturesque city like Escondido, speechless was probably the best way to describe our reaction when we first arrived in Mendota, which incidentally is known as the Cantaloupe Capital of the World. My first impression of Mendota was that it seemed to look something like a cross between a dusty small Texas border town and an old turn-of-the-century Wild West boomtown; we now found ourselves in this small town with literally no traffic lights, no treelined streets, no cultural civic center, no hospital, no high school, no McDonald's, no Burger King, no anything! What it did have were seventeen bars and nineteen small churches. I really began to think that, in fact, it might not actually be true, what one of my friends back home (who was quite familiar with Mendota) had jokingly said: "Mendota is God's country because only God could bear to live there."

We found out that Mendota's population was about 7,500 people, so we figured that with the town being so small, it would not be hard at all to find the church. Well, after a long and fruitless search, I guessed it was true that men don't ever think of asking for directions. We finally parked to make a small prayer, asking God to help us find the church. Sure enough, after about fifteen minutes, we happened to stop by this house where a young man was watering his lawn. With a big smile, Brother Paul Corchado told us that, in fact, he was a member of the church and would be more than glad to direct us there.

As I have mentioned at the beginning of this chapter, regarding my first impression of Mendota, while Mendota may not have the amenities of a city or even a large town, its greatest asset is its people. While these folks may not represent the upper echelons of the society, they are the most decent and hardworking "salt of the earth" people you can ever meet. Most folks in Mendota work in agriculture, whether it be harvesting in the fields, driving tractor, changing irrigation lines, or working at the numerous packing houses, and because of this, one thing is for sure, that they are a hardy and stable people.

Meeting the congregation was something very special for Tabitha and me. After the ceremony in which I took over the responsibility of the church as its pastor, they had a welcome luncheon. Wouldn't you know it, the food that was served was the type of food that could only be described as truly fatteningly delicious. It just so happened that when we were seated next to one of the members, Brother Francisco Adame, he saw me staring at his bowl of fish soup. I really did not care for fish soup, but he offered me some. Then all of a sudden, without any warning, coming from the middle of the bowl, a fish head bobbed up; I could have sworn that the eyes on that fish head were looking straight at me. I kindly thanked him but told him, "No, thank you." The congregation on that first Sunday consisted of about thirty-three people of which more than half were children.

The one first thing that I noticed when we had our first church meeting was that this congregation had really been hurt. They had gone through a series of pastors that just seemed to not be able to get along with the congregation. Unfortunately, some of these pastors had either been mean and abusive or, in some cases, downright dishonest. Secondly, this small congregation had such a low self-esteem because it was considered by many of the larger neighboring churches as a hole-in-the-wall church. Thirdly, the thing that most touched my heart was this congregation's great desire to want to build a new sanctuary. With so many promises that have been made and broken, so much hope that had been crumpled into disappointment, this small congregation found itself in deep despair. I spent the first couple of months doing my best to try to restore in them their confidence in the ministry. Because of all that this congregation had been through, you would have thought that there was no more life in them, but I am glad to say that this church was spunky and resilient and was ready to rise to the occasion. The very first thing that I felt I needed to do was to let them know that God had put in my heart a heavy burden and a strong desire to help them, with God's help, find a way to fulfill their thirteen-year dream of having their new sanctuary.

I do not mind telling you that I was afraid, because I knew that this was going to be the type of challenge that a young and inexperienced pastor like me would have to be crazy to take on. But it was not about me; it was about them and the fact that God could make it happen for them because of their determination and faith. Because of my perceived shortcomings as a young pastor, I learned very early on how much I really needed to be completely dependent on the mercy and leading of the Almighty God. The first thing that I felt from God that I should do was to write an article and publish it in the Opinion section of the *Firebaugh-Mendota Journal* (which was published only on Wednesdays). The article was entitled "The Little Church with the Big Dream." I wanted the community, the congregation, God, and especially, the devil to know that I really believed that by the hand of the Almighty God, this congregation would be granted their new sanctuary. The reason for my faith was that I had been mentored by a great man of God by the name of Pastor David Hernandez of Family Life Center in Los Angeles, who taught me, from the time he set me aside as a deacon to the time that I was ordained, the importance of dreaming big and having faith (with works) so that God would be able to do the impossible.

We decided to pattern our strategy after the story in the Bible of the prophet Nehemiah, who felt such a burden to rebuild the walls of Jerusalem that he went into a time of fasting and prayer, asking God to grant him and Israel a way to rebuild the walls. In those days, anybody who tried to talk to the king without his permission would be executed, but because of the consecration that he and the elders did, it was the king who approached Nehemiah and asked him what was troubling him. When the king heard Nehemiah's desire and the plight of God's people, he put himself at the disposition of Nehemiah. This was exactly what I told the congregation, that we needed to do this in order to get God's attention, so we started a chain of fasting and prayer every day that continued on for the next three years, including, whenever possible, a Sunday morning sunrise service. I also explained to them the importance that we all should be in one accord, as was the church in the book of Acts when the power of the Holy Ghost fell down. Things began to happen very quickly, and our church began to experience tremendous growth to the point that we went from Sunday services with 30 people to Sunday services with over 120 people—to God be the honor and the glory.

CHAPTER 3

City Hall

WITH THE CONTINUING growth of our congregation, we turned our attention to the task at hand. We started looking for a new location where we could either purchase a building to rehabilitate or a lot in which to build a new sanctuary. We found what we thought was going to be our new building when we were offered an old dance hall in the middle of the town. We started to negotiate with Joe Gomez, the owner, and came up with a reasonable price. We then inquired with city hall for the necessary steps to pull a conditional-use permit. We made sure in our agreement with Joe Gomez that the purchase of the building be conditional upon the approval of the conditional-use permit by the planning commission. This was, for many of those in our congregation, their first experience to deal with the city hall. After we filled out the conditional-use permit application, we made an appointment to appear before the planning commission to present our project. I drew a simple floor plan and a plan of action on how we planned to rehabilitate the building. I asked the congregation to make sure that everybody would appear with us when we presented our petition to the planning commission; needless to say, the hall was filled with everybody from the church the night we presented our case. There was an air of excitement in the place as we made our presentation to the planning commission. They were more than glad to orientate us on what we further needed to do to make this project happen, because this old building had been a visual blight to the town for many years. They instructed the building inspector to assist us in any way he could to make sure that we would comply with all the conditions that had been set forth.

After weeks of preparation and hard work, we were finally able to put together a plan that met all the conditions the planning commission had set forth. We made sure that everybody from the congregation was there for that second meeting, and again, there seemed to be an air of excitement because our congregation was ready to make this wonderful project a reality. What really touched my heart was that when the chairman of the planning commission noted that in all the years he had been involved with the planning commission, he had never seen such a united group like our congregation. He then proceeded to announce that our conditional-use permit had been approved, to which our congregation gave a standing ovation. What was more amazing was that the planning commission in turn gave our congregation a standing ovation. God is good and greatly to be praised.

When I met with Mr. Gomez and presented him the conditional-use permit and told him we were ready to purchase the property from him, I was shocked when he responded that he had changed his mind. I was totally devastated by this and felt so terrible that I would have to give our congregation the bad news, that after all the hard work that we had been put into this endeavor, Mr. Gomez had changed his mind. We contacted everybody and set up a church meeting for the next Tuesday night to notify them of the terrible news. As I drove to the church, I was apprehensive of what the reaction of the congregation might be, and I really felt bad that I had let them down. As I stepped into the church, the first thing I noticed was that I could hear everybody singing and seeming to be having a good time. As I stood up to give them the bad news, I feared that there would be a lot of disillusioned and upset people. To my shock and amazement, instead of being sad and discouraged, the members told me that though this building was not meant to be ours, they felt such a sense of excitement that they had not felt for many years. They told me that they had faith that God would answer us and give us another place. This gave me great encouragement and strength, but I had no idea that we were just beginning to see the hand of God in our lives. Unbeknownst to me, many of the people in both the planning commission and those that had been present in the meetings would shortly become great factors in what God planned to do for us. This experience has made us understand how God truly works in wonderful and mysterious ways.

RICHARD MEZA

CHAPTER 4

Juanita Avenue

As WE CONTINUED our fasting and prayers, and with the rapid growth of our congregation, the dream of a new sanctuary burned even more deeply within our hearts. I would tell the congregation every Sunday night that I knew the Lord would answer us. There was a real air of expectation that things were now really beginning to move. After we looked for a suitable property for months, the property actually came looking for us. I received a note from Brother José Marquez with the name and phone number of Elizabeth Gomez. When I called Elizabeth, she told me that she and her fiancé had heard that our church was looking for a property and that they had been trying to track me down. We went to look at the property, and I knew right away that this was where God wanted His temple to be built. Please understand that as a young and inexperienced pastor, I did not have the luxury of taking anything for granted, so I went before the Lord and asked him to confirm whether or not this was the property that He had for us. Remember, I told you from the beginning I was completely and totally dependent on the leading of God, because unlike many of the spiritual giants of our times, I had neither the experience nor the spiritual sensitivity of these great men and women of faith. But one thing that I did have was a simple faith in the God that I served. Over the years, I had developed this simple faith, along with a keen sense of spiritual instinct, through trial and error under the supervision of my pastor, David Hernandez.

The property was on the north side of town, right next to where a brand housing project was to be built, but more important was the fact that this property at 636 Juanita Avenue was already developed, including curb and gutter. Many people do not realize that one of the most expensive phases in any construction is the development of the curb and gutter portion, which can easily run into thousands of dollars. This is the wonderful thing about God; when He sees that you are totally dependent on Him, He will move mountains for you. While it wasn't just the fasting and the prayer (because our faith was not in fasting and prayers but in the God to whom we pray and fast), the fact is that like Nehemiah, our congregation had gone into a time of consecration and that in every service, we would worship God and let him know how much we needed him. I believe that this touched God's heart to the point that he was ready to start moving mountains for our small but spunky congregation.

With God's help and the consent of the congregation, I came to an agreement with them to purchase the property for $45,000. The terms of the agreement were that the sale would be final, contingent upon the city of Mendota approving a conditional-use permit allowing for a place of worship to be erected on the property. Furthermore, the agreement stated that we would give them a $10,000 down payment and pay a monthly interest-only payment of $300 per month until the project was completed and final funding was secured. Truly, only God could open the door of opportunity in such an awesome manner. In a short time, with what we had in the bank and with a little help from the congregation, we were able to hand over the deposit and turn our attention toward preparing for the building of our new sanctuary. The wonderful thing that happened was that we all got together and came up with a $10,000 deposit, some of which came from about $8,000 that was left in our fund. I spent the day before escrow closed counting everything, including rolls of quarters, dimes, nickels, and pennies. Then the day after escrow closed, we received a refund of about $70.17.

With the acquisition of the property now in hand, the next task was to ensure the property was properly marked and fenced. Because of the construction that was occurring close to the property, I was able to find a surveyor who, for a nominal charge, marked the boundaries of our new property. Next, through a referral of one of the brothers in the congregation, I was able to find a small independent fencing company that was able to install a chain-link fence around the whole property for about $1,400. It seemed that everywhere we turned, God opened some very important doors for us, and it seemed to be happening at the right

RICHARD MEZA

time. There seemed to be a growing sense of purpose and confidence in our congregation that felt like nothing would go wrong. The truth was that we had no idea what was coming next, but one thing was for sure, whatever needed to happen, only God could make it happen.

We had finally arrived at what we had been asking for, a property on which we would be able to build our sanctuary. We were ready to build; the only problem was that now we had little money and almost no resources to build it with. All our money had been put into securing the property, so it seemed like we were at an impasse. So the whole congregation met at the new property, and we all walked around the perimeter and prayed in the name of Jesus Christ for God's blessings. What you have to understand is that when God is ready to move, all of man's wisdom and sense of timing is thrown out on his ear, because after all the years that this little church had wanted for God to grant their congregation their dream of building a new sanctuary, coupled with the years of continual fasting and prayer, I believe they had touched the heart of God. Money or no money, resources or no resources, God was about to answer in a mighty and powerful way.

CHAPTER 5

Thursday Night Service

AS MOST MIDWEEK services usually go, ours was no exemption. We only had a few folks attending on this certain Thursday night service, yet for no reason that I can remember, I felt compelled to go outside and stand at the corner of Eighth Street and Quince Street. You need to understand that because Mendota is a very small town, to stand at the corner during midweek at about seven thirty in the evening does not make any sense at all, because there is virtually no traffic coming through at that time. As I have stated earlier, I am not, nor have I ever been, a mystical preacher. I have never seen a bright light, have never seen an angel (though I would love to), nor have I ever heard an audible voice; but I do know one thing, that when God speaks to me, it's usually in a still small voice, as described in 1 Kings 19, and it was in that still small voice that the Lord spoke to me and asked me to stand in that corner. Sure enough, after standing there for about five minutes, I saw a white Chrysler New Yorker automobile slowly pulling up right in front of me and coming to a stop. Then as I saw the power window roll down, somebody called out to me and asked me if I was the pastor of the church. I stooped down a little bit to take a better look at whom I was talking to, and to my surprise, it was none other than Mr. Thurman Alexander along with his wife, Jeanette. I had first met Mr. Alexander when he was present at the planning commission meetings during the time that our church was first looking into buying that old dance hall building. Though that project never came to pass, as God would have it, Mr. Alexander happened to be the interim building inspector during that process. As I had mentioned in the prior chapter, God had used that occasion to introduce our church to Mr. Alexander. It shows you how God works in mysterious and wonderful ways. "I heard you were thinking about building a church," Mr. Alexander commented. "I was wondering if you could use a little help." I just could not believe my ears how God had placed this wonderful man in our path. We agreed to meet for lunch in a couple of days at Jack's Steakhouse in the town of Firebaugh. I was pleased because this would give me some time to come up with a strategy of how we could work with Mr. Alexander on building the sanctuary. I was confident I could wow him with my surefire approach during our power lunch, but God had other plans.

After a good steak-sandwich lunch, I showed him the basic floor plan design I felt God had shown me for the sanctuary, which was based partially on the available lot space. It was right then and there that I decided to go for the kill; I explained very carefully to him that with our ladies auxiliary group selling tamales, the best we would be able to offer him in compensation to head the construction project would be about $200 per week, tops. He looked me square in the eye and asked me if I remembered him ever asking me for any type of salary. I admitted that he had not, then he told me, "Furthermore, Preach [that was what Mr. Alexander decided to call me], the only thing I asked you was if you wanted some help or not." When I humbly replied that we could surely use his help, he responded, "Then let's get busy!" Just like that, God had sent to our little church a retired millionaire contractor who, for the next seven months, donated not only his time and expertise but also the use of his general contractor license and the use, at no charge, of his forklift, backhoe, skip loader, and various other equipment, specialty tools, and implements! He would not accept any money, not even a dime, to cover his fuel expenses. Truly, God had begun to shine upon our little church in a mighty and powerful way!

CHAPTER 6

The Ball Gets Rolling

ONE OF THE most difficult and expensive phases of any construction project is the making of the plans. As I had already mentioned, I had an idea in mind of what I perceived to be the floor plan that I believe God wanted for the sanctuary. But this is when you really and truly want to make sure you're listening to the voice of God, for this is the one truly good principle to follow when approaching such an important and serious endeavor.

I had already had a bad experience a few months before when during a big service involving a number of churches that was held in a brand-new, beautiful sanctuary that had recently been built, I requested that it be announced at the end of the service that our church was looking for help to find an architect to draw up our plans. After the service, the pastor of this new sanctuary came up to me and started to ask me some questions. Interpreting this as genuine concern on his part, I filled him in with all the details, but I was so shocked and disappointed by his response. Instead of offering me any type of encouragement, he began scolding me by telling me that I was just a dumb and inexperienced young pastor who was way over his head. He told me that I had no idea what I was doing, and based on his experience (it took them many years to build their sanctuary), I was crazy to even think that I could break ground this year or even in the next couple of years. I just stood there completely devastated, not knowing exactly what to do or think. I had just been told off by a man of God who had just successfully finished building a huge sanctuary with the capacity of 1,400 people. The saying "Back to the drawing board" rang in my ears as I headed back home, feeling both defeated and disappointed.

The one thing I have learned over the years is that man's wisdom is not God's wisdom. I count it as an advantage that, because I was so young and inexperienced, I instinctively called upon the only one individual that I knew I could trust during this difficult time—my heavenly Father. With all my heart and with all the emotion I felt, this young pastor called out to God and expressed to Him how deeply devastated I felt. I told Him of the hurt and discouragement I felt at being rebuked by this man of God but also of the despair that I felt from continuing to hit wall after wall in trying to accomplish what I felt He wanted me to do. God just loves it when you let it all hang out because it shows Him that you are truly and completely dependent upon Him for everything. This is when God is at His best, and this is when things can truly begin to happen. I do not want to keep repeating myself, but because I am dedicating this book not only to my family, friends, and the congregation but also to every young and inexperienced pastor who is *foolish* enough to believe that God can do the impossible, remember that God's greatest miracles are truly manifested more often in ordinary circumstances and that God almost always prefers to communicate with us through that still small voice that is mentioned in 1 Kings 19.

It was that "still small voice" that encouragingly let me know I was doing the right thing, that though I was not following man's wisdom and common sense, as long as I continued to seek God's face in prayer and fasting—in other words, personal consecration—and as long as I continued in faith, backed up with works, God had everything under control. It was shortly after this experience that things began to unfold very rapidly as God began to open doors.

CHAPTER 7

The Plans

THE EVENTS THAT I am about to recount to you are going to seem incredible, but I want to assure you that this is really the way it has all happened. While we were waiting for the approval of the conditional-use permit, based on the floor plan we had submitted, Mr. Alexander instructed me to rent a Ditch Witch. A Ditch Witch is a trenching machine that allows you to dig the footings needed for the foundation of the church building. He told me exactly what I had to do as far as how wide and deep the ditch needed to be then told me that once I was done, I needed to call him so he could go and inspect the work. After taking about two days to complete the task, once I was done, I called Mr. Alexander, but there was no response. After attempting to contact him for most of the day, I even went by his house, but because nobody was home, I just waited by the phone, praying that I would eventually hear from him. Later that day, I received a call from his wife that apparently, Mr. Alexander had been rushed to the hospital. She told me that he had suffered a stroke and that she would be in contact with me the next day. When I hung up, I felt completely overwhelmed, thinking how in the world we would be able to even start the construction if the one person we needed the most might well now be out of the picture.

Early the next day, I headed to the property to talk to the surveyor. When I could not find him, I went to one of the model homes to see if somebody had seen him. As I stepped into the home, I saw a group of men that were gathered around a table, discussing some plans. When they told me they had not seen him, I thanked them and headed out to search elsewhere. You can only imagine what was going through my mind, which was full of worry and distress because of what was happening with Mr. Alexander. Just as I stepped out of the house, one of the men, who had apparently followed me out, tapped me on the shoulder and started to talk to me. He asked me if I was Richard Meza, the pastor of the apostolic church that was about to be built. When I responded that I was, right there in broad daylight, he broke down and started to sob. When he gathered himself, he told me his name was Little Joe Rodriguez and that God had told him to let me know that everything was going to be all right. He told me he was a cement contractor and that he and his crew were at our service. Once Little Joe Rodriguez left, I kind of just stood there with tears in my eyes and with a heart full of gratitude that God had gone out of His way to assure me that everything would be all right.

The next day, I, in fact, did get a call from Mrs. Alexander, telling me that Mr. Alexander wanted to see me right away. I put on my dress clothes because I was just going to go visit him and pray for him. When I got there, Mr. Alexander told me that not only had he suffered a stroke but that they also had to resuscitate him three times. As I got ready to offer him words of encouragement and to make a prayer for him, he interrupted me and told me, "What are you doing, Preach?" He told me to put him in his truck and take him to inspect the footings I had dug. When we got there, he instructed me to take out a chair and a parasol he had in the back of his truck. Once I sat him down, from a distance, he inspected my work and then told me to take out the shovel, which he also had in the back of his truck. When I asked him if it was okay for me to go home and change my clothes, he told me, "You don't have time, Preach. Get into that hole and get to work now!" I did not hesitate; I jumped into the trench, dress clothes and all, and started cleaning out the sides of the walls. Even when I gashed my hand, he told me not to stop; instead, he had me tape up my hand with some clear tape he had in his truck. Finally, when one of the brothers went by, I asked him to go fetch me some work clothes, but I did not mind working because God had shown me that no matter what, He was with us. To God be the honor and the glory.

Shortly thereafter, I met with Little Joe Rodriguez and a city civil engineer he had recommended to help us develop our building plans. Later on, we had a meeting at the old church with Mr. Alexander, Joe Lyons (an architect recommended by Mr. Alexander), Little Joe

Rodriguez, and the civil engineer. At the meeting, all the details were worked out and the final design of the building was decided on, but the most wonderful thing of all was that the cost to draw up the plans was only going to be $2,500. Please understand that plans for a project of this scope, which had been quoted by another architect, were somewhere between $12,000 and $15,000; truly, God was on our side. But even the $2,500 was a major undertaking for our small congregation because of all the monies we had already spent. I got together with the church, and with about $1,300 we had left in our fund and with whatever else we all were able to muster, we were able to come up with the money. When I met the civil engineer at his door to hand him the money, as he saw me counting it out, including the coins, he stopped me and looked visibly touched, and with tears in his eyes, he told me that it was not necessary to count it out, that he knew it was all there. After he thanked me and closed his door, I could see that he had also felt what I had felt at the moment: we had both felt the presence of God.

CHAPTER 8

Construction Begins (or Does It?)

I N A SHORT time, the plans were completed and were then submitted to the city of Mendota for plan check and approval. I believe because God had allowed us to have already gone through the process when we attempted to purchase that old dance hall building from Joe Gomez, God had us find favor with both the planning commission and also with one very important individual—none other than Mr. Thurman Alexander, who had been the interim building inspector that first time. The planning commission speedily preapproved the conditional-use permit, with final approval contingent upon the final okay by the city engineer, which was when things really began to get interesting. At first, I really could not figure out Mr. G (this is what I am going call the city engineer because when I first met him, he seemed like a really nice person). As I began to deal with him, I began to get the feeling that he would fight giving us the final okay to this project to the very end. Even after we had made the numerous corrections and modifications he had required, he still kept on adding other conditions that we needed to meet because everything needed to be done by the book. The final hurdle was the number of parking spaces required for the sanctuary. Even though he could have easily made an exception by granting a perfectly legal variance, he stuck to his guns and would not budge. Even after the planning commission instructed him to resolve the situation, he stated that as city engineer, he was well within his authority to insist that the number of parking spaces required be adhered to.

What I am about to tell you that happened next is an event that you will have to draw your own conclusions about. It was during this time that Mr. G suffered a stroke that left him incapacitated for about two to three weeks. When he finally came back to work, he was told again by the planning commission and the city manager (in no uncertain terms) to come up with a legally acceptable compromise that would satisfy the number of parking spaces required. He finally relented and came up with a compromise, after so many delays, which gave us final approval to get started. And oh, by the way, we were informed shortly thereafter that Mr. G had been terminated.

New church under construction

RICHARD MEZA

CHAPTER 9

The Unstoppable Wave

L IKE AN UNSTOPPABLE tsunami, door after door began to be opened by God in swift and awesome succession. Things begin to happen very quickly as the following events that I'm about to recount to you began unfolding in such a manner that it was quite evident that God's hand was involved.

On the day before the actual concrete pouring of the foundation was to happen, I sat on a bench at the property all by myself, just contemplating the monumental challenges that were before us, and frankly, I wondered how God was going to pull this off. As I sat there, Ron Corliss, the city manager for Mendota, interrupted my thoughts and asked if he could sit down. After congratulating me on the project, he then asked me what my plan of action was and how the funding was coming along. After I explained to him how God was directing me to go forward and to trust in Him for everything, Ron just looked at me as if I were crazy. To tell you the truth, as I sat there, I could not have agreed more with him. How in the world did I ever think that we could pull this stunt off, the building of the church sanctuary with no money? But this is where, in hindsight, I realize that it wasn't me pulling off any type of stunt, but rather, this was God's magnificent plan to answer a prayer of many years for a small group of people who dared to believe in the power of the Almighty God and, at the same time, for God to confound the wise man.

Anybody with any sense will tell you that you never ever attempt to start any building project unless the funding is in place, and you absolutely have to make sure you have a business plan in place. To do otherwise is simply inviting disaster. You are taking a great risk because the worst thing that can happen to any building construction project is for it to run out of money. Almost always, once a building project stops because of the lack of funds, it almost never starts again. Furthermore, whenever I travelled into the city of Fresno, I would always have to pass by an all-too-real reminder of this; I would pass by an abandoned old lot on which you could see that someone had built a cement foundation, and there was, on one corner of the lot, a sign, which had fallen down, that proclaimed that this lot was going to be the future home of a certain church. It was a stark and grim reminder of failed dreams, poor planning, and defeat; because of this, God knew that I did everything in my power and ability beforehand to try to develop a plausible business plan and to secure funding. But in this case, God had other plans; He literally took the project out of my hands and put it into His own hands so that, as quoted in the Bible, "no man may say it was by his hand, but instead it was by the hand of the Lord." I turned to Ron Corliss and asked him, since he certainly must know people with money, to please ask around to see if there would be anybody interested in helping our church. As he left, he promised me he would try to do his best. I thanked him for whatever he could do for us and headed home to rest and to prepare for whatever was going to happen the next day.

Prior to that, I also found out that we needed hundreds of cubic yards of sand to be able to level out not only the foundation but also the rest of the property; this was itself a daunting challenge because the cost of so much cubic yards of sand would be astronomical. So as a congregation, we did the only thing that we could do—we went to the Lord. I felt from the Lord that we should contact the ready-mix concrete company we were going to purchase sand from for our foundation and explain to them our situation. God moved in a mighty way in that because we were to purchase the cement from them; they allowed us to go to the same riverbank that they get their sand from and get all the cubic yards of sand that we needed. We did this with the help of one of Mr. Alexander's friends, who retrieved all the sand, in multiple trips, by using his dump truck at no charge.

The next day turned out to be what could only be described as a flurry of activity, but the day before, God had already started to do some wonderful things for us. First, after Ron had left as the day drew to a close, there were a few of us who watered down and tamped the

RICHARD MEZA

sand to assure that the ground would be good and hard for the concrete pouring. But time began to gain on us, as the sun was going down, and because the kind neighbor that usually allowed us to use her electricity was not home, we were running out of daylight to complete the work. I am telling you that the members of our church just did not know the word *quit*; they began to bring in their cars and trucks right up to the area and turned on their headlights, and as more vehicles began to arrive, including a couple of ice cream trucks, before we knew it, we had more than enough light to finish the task. I know the Bible says that the Creator said, "Let there be light," and there was light, but the Lord sure works in mysterious ways. My God is an awesome God!

Years before I arrived in Mendota, one of the members of our church, Sister Blanca Gallardo, had given to her church, with all her heart, a tithe donation of $25,000 due to a life insurance policy settlement she had received because of the untimely death of her husband. Because of this donation, the congregation, I was told, really felt optimistic that one day God would grant them a new sanctuary. Unfortunately, things did not go as planned; though the pastor at that time did put a small cement walkway around the church, apparently, he used some of the funds for his personal gain. This thoroughly discouraged the congregation, and eventually, this, along with some other unfortunate events, led to the pastor resigning from the church. Unfortunately, by the time I got to Mendota, the damage was already done. I could literally feel the disillusionment that Sister Blanca Gallardo and the rest of the congregation felt toward the ministry, most especially with the pastor. Yet that night, I felt from God to ask her and her husband, Brother Frank Gallardo, to take a leap of faith. I asked them to please loan the church $11,000 to pay for the cement. I did this for two reasons: I did it because God told me to and, secondly, because I knew the Lord would help them to heal, and this would restore their confidence in the ministry. They did loan us the money, and I am proud to say that a few months later, the loan was paid in full. My God is an awesome God!

Also, first and foremost, true to his word, Little Joe Rodriguez was there for us when we most needed him. He had his seasoned and experienced cement crew ready to jump into action. The most amazing thing was that he did not charge us one penny at all; the only thing he asked for was that we feed his crew. I was so excited that I literally could not contain myself because I felt like jumping, screaming, crying, and laughing all at the same time. It took all my strength to preserve my decorum and dignity because I felt so overjoyed and so profoundly thankful to God for the miracles that he was doing.

When the next day finally arrived, everybody was ready to make it happen. The strategy was to roll out the wire mesh as the cement-mixing trucks began to unload the cement, with Little Joe Rodriguez's crew laying it down, the rest of us supporting them. As one after another of the cement-mixing truck started coming in, with a total of nineteen trucks by the end of the day, everybody jumped into action. As I got into the action, helping with whatever I could, I noticed that everybody seemed to be working together in harmony; it just seemed to me like the Holy Ghost had it all under control. While I was in the thick of things, either helping or most likely just getting in the way, I thought I heard somebody calling out for me. When I turned toward the direction of the voice, I was surprised to see Ron Corliss, the city manager, running toward me. I was further surprised to see that he had tears in his eyes as he then gave me a big bear hug and told me the most amazing news. He said, "God has answered your prayers. I found somebody willing to donate all of your construction materials!" The next day, Mr. Alexander and I sat down and put together a complete list of all the needed materials, including all the wood studs, half-inch drywall sheets, electrical wiring and fittings, all the anchors, and even the nails we would need to get started. Sure enough, two weeks later, I beheld the most beautiful sight I had ever seen, as I saw a brand-new semi-rig roll into our construction site with two trailers full of all the donated materials we had requested. The most wonderful thing is that this is why the scripture states in Proverbs 33:3, "Call upon me, and I will show you great and mighty things you have not seen."

Many wonderful things happened during the next few weeks and months, but the most wonderful of all this was the fact that God was answering the one petition that this small but determined congregation had been asking and crying out to the Lord for so many years—God was granting them their dream of a new sanctuary, because God always answers prayer.

Dump truck loaded with sand for the church constructions

One of the 19 cement trucks that brought cement that day

Cement foundation of the church being laid.

CHAPTER 10

Good Help Is Easy to Find

WHILE WE KNEW we were in good hands under the direction of Mr. Alexander and that everybody in the congregation was willing to donate as much time and effort as possible, the fact remained that we would eventually need some skilled people to help us with the different facets involved in this type of construction project. One day, as I inspected the property, an individual come up to me and introduced himself. He told me his name was Baudelio Gonzalez and that he lived right across the street. Thinking he was just being a good neighbor, I thanked him and told him that whenever he had some free time, we could definitely use his help. He just stood there for a moment and told me that I did not understand; he was not only offering to help us once in a while but was also committed to helping us see the construction of the building all the way through. I looked at him and asked him why, and his response really surprised me. He told me that at one time, when he found himself in a very difficult and challenging situation, he promised the Lord that if God would help him out of his predicament, he would help build a church somewhere without charging one penny. When God responded to his petition and he was allowed to return to his family, he was amazed that God had placed this church construction project right across the street from his house. Just like that, God gave us a skilled carpenter with many years of experience who would help us achieve our dream of building this new sanctuary. As you will see in later chapters, Baudelio was only one in a long line of skilled people God sent to help build our sanctuary.

CHAPTER 11

The Nightmare Begins

I STILL REMEMBER the night it all began as if it were last night. Maybe you have heard about how a tragedy is something that happens to somebody else, that is, until it comes knocking at your door. Tragedy came knocking at our door on October 30, 1989, when Tabitha and my two children—my daughter, Ashly, aged five years, and my son, Richie, aged five months—and I were spending the night at my mother's house in Los Angeles, California. We had been in service at the Escondido Apostolic Church, where Pastor Philemon Anaya had graciously lifted up a love offering for our church construction project. Somewhere around 11:00 p.m., I heard the baby cry, and I noticed that Tabitha did not get up to check on Richie like she always would. When I went to check on the baby, I was taken aback to see Tabitha in the throes of a grand mal seizure; this type of seizure is one of the worst seizures anybody can have because it causes your body to spasm violently.

While my mother took care of the children, Tabitha and I were transported by ambulance to the nearest hospital, which happened to be Kaiser Permanente on Sunset Boulevard in Hollywood, California. During the ride to the hospital and even when she was admitted, Tabitha kept getting these grand mal seizures; in fact, the seizures did not stop until they were able to stabilize her. After being admitted through triage in the emergency department, she was finally admitted into a multibed room. After taking care of all the admitting paperwork, I went upstairs to see how she was doing. The minute I stepped into the room, I could literally feel the spirit of death. Please do not judge me for what I am about to say and what I've ended up doing. During my ministry, I have had to deal with a lot of death, God only knows why, so I know only too well when the spirit of death is present. The other patient in the room was a gentle soul who was in the last stages of terminal cancer; her eyes were sunken in, and her lips were pursed back so that, in essence, she looked like a living corpse. All I knew was that I needed to get my wife out of the room, so I went and talked to the nurse in charge. She explained to me that because it was the night shift, staff was limited, so it would be quite a while before they would be able to have Tabitha moved to another room. Because of what I felt, I was insistent that Tabitha be moved immediately to another room, and finally, after pleading my case, I was able to convince her to have Tabitha moved to another room with my help.

Once we were in the new room, I was finally able to talk to her for a few minutes, and it just broke my heart to see her reaction; she quietly wept because aside from worrying about our kids, she also felt so devastated because of what she had just been through. She was also worried about the future of our church, because when this happened, the walls had already been erected and the work was just getting started. I encouraged her by reminding her that the Word of God said that all things would work for the good of those that love God, and if there was anybody in this universe who loved God, it was definitely her. After we prayed for God to give her strength, for the first time since she suffered her first seizure, Tabitha was finally able to fall into a deep sleep. Later that night, she was put through a battery of tests to try to determine what was causing her severe epileptic seizures. As the hours dragged on, the devil worked overtime on me, trying to cause me to lose my composure. I had negative thoughts, like "How are you going to pay for the thousands of dollars this is going to cost you? Who is going to take care of your children if Tabitha becomes incapacitated or, worse, if she dies? What about the church building project? How are you going to be able to continue that?" To make matters worse, I became aware as we left for this trip that one of the ministers in our church tried to undermine the project by going from house to house, creating discord among the members. As my head throbbed, I really felt like I was going crazy. This was when I found out how great and merciful our God truly was, because He, in that still small voice, assured me through the Holy Ghost that He had it all under control. I could hear God whispering to me that no matter what, He would give us the strength and understanding to overcome whatever circumstances

RICHARD MEZA

might lie ahead. The sense of calm and profound peace that I felt at that moment was only surpassed by the tremendous strength the Lord gave me in that hospital that night. I give God all the honor and all the glory because He saw our need and reached all the way down into that hospital and gave me exactly what I needed; this is where I come to understand what Psalms 121 means when it reads, "My help comes from the Lord, who makes the heavens and the earth." Even as I write about this experience so many years later, I cannot help but feel emotional and thankful for what the Lord has done for us.

In the morning, we received the news that an x-ray had shown a dark spot on the left side of her brain and that further analysis would be needed to confirm what they suspected, that Tabitha possibly had a brain tumor. But because we were indigent, we were told we would need to transport Tabitha back to Fresno so that she could be admitted into the county hospital called Valley Medical Center. In retrospect, we had no idea that the trip to Fresno would be the start of what is now a twenty-six-year journey of countless medical challenges.

CHAPTER 12

Halloween 1989

WE FINALLY ARRIVED in Fresno at about one in the afternoon on October 31, 1989, on, wouldn't you know, Halloween. My wife's sister and brother-in-law, Pastor Prospero and First Lady Esther Jacobo, took my daughter and my son back to Mendota with them so that I could just concentrate on Tabitha. Thus began what would be our more than twenty-six-year journey of countless surgeries, seizures, radiation treatments, strokes and countless doctors, neurologists, neurosurgeons, and nurses who had helped me and my wife throughout our journey. When we entered the emergency department of Fresno County Valley Medical Center, the first thing I noticed was that because it was Halloween, it was extremely busy and crowded, as most county hospitals tended to be at this time of the year. In the midst of the long lines, commotion, and noise, I was able to commandeer a wheelchair for Tabitha, then I sat down and filled out what seemed to be a ton of endless paperwork. After she was ushered through the nurses' triage station, which had been set up because of the tremendous number of people that kept streaming in, I was told to go to the waiting room until her name was called. But because the waiting room was just too crowded, I had to find a spot where we could sit and wait. I spied an unoccupied gurney alongside one of the aisles, so I laid Tabitha on it, and with a chair that I was able to secure, we sat down and just waited, and waited, and waited for what seemed to be an eternity. All afternoon and into the evening, being that it was Halloween, we saw all kinds of people brought in—everyone from gunshot, accident, and crime victims to people that were so sick that they were screaming in pain and throwing up all over the place. I would not wish for anybody to experience what we saw that night, so many people hurt or disfigured or with such extreme injuries that it would just boggle the mind.

We waited in the aisle from about one o'clock in the afternoon until seven the next morning. I do not mind telling you that it was the longest and most excruciating sixteen hours of waiting we had ever experienced in our lives. Tabitha was finally taken in for an MRI, then we had to wait for a couple of more hours for the results. The news was not good at all, because the MRI confirmed that the large mass in her brain was definitely a tumor. She was admitted into the hospital and finally into a room where we waited for the next step. Shortly after that, a Dr. Cooper came in and introduced himself as our neurosurgeon and informed us what the next step would be, which was to perform a biopsy to see what type of tumor we were dealing with. I want to comment that though Dr. Cooper was small in stature, he seemed like a giant to us, with this wonderful bedside manner, and we will always appreciate so much his considerate yet frank approach with us. When the results came back, Dr. Cooper came in to inform us that they thought there was a possibility that the tumor was malignant. It hit me like a ton of bricks, as had happened at Kaiser, how in the world I was going to be able to handle this terrible situation. I felt so overwhelmed by the magnitude of the situation that I did not know whether to run, shout, or cry, so I just stood there like a lifeless statue. I just did not know what to do. Here we were smack in the middle of the church construction project, with no money, and with two children to worry about and an uncertain future regarding my wife. There is a scripture in Psalm 122 that reads, "My help comes from the Lord who made the heavens and the earth." This means that no matter how impossible your situation may seem, things that are impossible for man are all possible for God. This means that no matter how impossible your situation may seem, God has everything under control. At that very moment, I felt such a spirit of calmness, peace, and strength come over me that even now, twenty-six years later, I cannot help but swell up with tears of profound gratitude with my God. I want to emphasize that, as I have tried to point out during the writing of this book, I take great pains in making sure I am not glossing over anything at all. As I stood in that hospital, I was this very young and very scared pastor with all types of insecurities and fears. That the Lord, at that moment, chose to have mercy on me and that he came down and blessed and comforted me so much, all I can say is blessed be the name of the Lord; my God is an awesome God.

By the next time we met with Dr. Cooper, quite a few things had transpired. Talk about emotional ups and downs. First of all, Tabitha was operated on to try to remove the brain tumor, but immediately after the operation, we were given some very disheartening news. When they went in to remove the tumor all they, they were able to find there was an abscess of some type of liquid, but because of the delicate area they were working on and because of Tabitha's continuing danger of epileptic seizures, they had no choice but to drain out the fluid and close the area up again. When the postoperation x-ray was taken, it showed that unfortunately, the tumor was still there. I felt like all my strength drained out of me, and I felt even worse when I had to give Tabitha the bad news. When I got to the room, there was my Tabitha in the hospital bed, just sobbing uncontrollably, because in order to perform the surgery, they had to shave off her beautiful long hair on the tumor side, but there was nothing we could do. Dr. Cooper came in and gave us the bad news that because time was so critical, they would have to go back in to remove the tumor.

CHAPTER 13

The Dead Church Experience

WITH THE PROSPECT of Tabitha having to have another operation, I headed back to Mendota to check on my kids and to see how things were going with the construction. I was a broken man in more ways than one because just as I feared, the progress of the construction had come almost to a stop because everybody's attention was on what was going to happen to my wife. The uncertainty was unnerving at best because as I have already mentioned, once a construction project begins, it is imperative that, in all costs, it does not stop.

I remember that the next morning, as I tried to attend to my children, something happened that even today still brings tears to my eyes. My five-year-old daughter, Ashly Elizabeth, whom I was prepping up for school, asked me to comb her hair. With me still dealing with the fact the my wife's life hung in the balance as she lay in that hospital bed at Valley Medical Center, I found myself struggling to even accomplish a simple task like combing her hair. I kept tangling up her hair to the point that she told me, "Daddy, don't comb it so hard. Comb like Mommy does!" I realized in that moment that I just did not know how to comb my little girl's hair. Ashly turned to me, with tears in her eyes, and told me something that still to this day reverberates in my heart. She said, "I miss my mommy." And it was at that moment I had never felt more hopeless in my life as I grabbed ahold of my poor daughter and held her tight while I fought back my own tears.

Just as I felt I was going to completely break down, in came my sister-in-law, First Lady Esther Jacobo, to help me with Ashly. I will never forget that if it were not for the kindness of her and her husband,

Pastor Prospero Jacobo, in helping me take care and feed my children, I just do not know what I would have done. To them and to God I owe a debt of gratitude.

From there I headed to our old church to try to clear my head because honestly, I continued to feel completely overwhelmed by our situation, because aside from Tabitha's health situation and the situation with the church construction, I literally had almost no money for gas or to feed my children. I entered the church, got on my knees, and started to pray to God with all my heart. The reason that I went to pray was that my pastor, David Hernandez, had taught me many years ago that in the midst of great crisis, we need to always go before the Lord and thank Him for His love and His mercy. Pastor Hernandez also taught me that we should always call upon the name of the Lord for everything because when we, as the scripture in 1 Peter 5:7 states, cast all our care upon him, he cares for us. I tell you the truth that when I went into our old church to pray, I absolutely did not feel like praying, much less worshiping God; I felt such a deadness in my heart, as if I were a lifeless statue. But the Word of God tells us that we walk not by sight, or feeling; we walk by faith (2 Cor. 5:7). So I began to thank God and worship Him for all that He had done for us. I thanked God for our children whom He had given to us. I thanked Him for my wonderful Tabitha, for the church that we were honored to pastor; all in all, I thanked Him for everything. Then I began to worship Him with everything that I had, including for my salvation, for the Holy Ghost, and for the strength He had been giving me. I worshiped Him and praised Him until I couldn't anymore because of exhaustion. I would love to tell you that after this, I felt some type of mystical or celestial release, but I felt pretty much the same way that I felt when I first came into the sanctuary—dead.

As I got up and got ready to leave the church, somebody knocked on the side door of the church. When I opened the door, I was very surprised to see a certain sister and her husband; in fact, these were the last people I would have expected to see. We had had our differences of opinion over some matters, and she had made no secret the fact she really resented me. But there she was, along with her husband. All of a sudden both she and her husband embraced me and told me that their prayers were with my family and me, then they handed me an envelope and told me that they were at my service. Talk about being speechless. I just could not believe it; all I can say is that God is always full of surprises.

But God wasn't done yet, as I found out when I left the church and went straight to Circle K to fill up my truck with gas from the love offering that those kind folks had given me. I figured I could at least fill up one of the two tanks on my F350 pickup truck, but as I sat in my truck, looking at the envelope, somebody knocked on my window. As I looked up, I recognized the young man who greeted me and asked me how I was doing. Without even waiting for a response from me, he told me to hold on for a second and then headed into the store. A few moments later, he came back and told me to go ahead and fill up my truck with gas. Even more amazing was the fact that after I filled up one of the tanks, he insisted I fill up the other tank. After I thanked him profusely, I just had to ask him why he had done that; his response was that because the Lord had told him to do it. Just like that, God had not only sent me encouragement but also supplied the immediate needs of my family. God is an awesome God.

CHAPTER 14

Back to the Hospital

I WANT TO acknowledge all the people and all the churches that prayed and fasted for us; their words of encouragement really meant so much to us. Believe me when I tell you that we could actually feel the intercessory prayers that were made on behalf of Tabitha and her family. I also want to thank my father- and mother-in-law, Pastor Silvestre and First Lady Eva Peña, both of whom have gone on to be with the Lord, for all their love and support in our time of trouble.

I still remember it as if it were yesterday when Dr. Cooper went into the room to talk to me about the next course of action for Tabitha. My father-in-law was on one side of the bed, while I was at the foot of the bed, when Dr. Cooper gave us some unbelievable news. He said the following to us: "Truly, God is answering the prayers that are being made because when we did the second biopsy on Tabitha, we did not find any evidence that her tumor is malignant." Now many skeptics may say that there may have been a mistake made during the first biopsy, but we choose to believe that God deserves all the honor and glory for the great miracle He has performed that day. Dr. Cooper said that the tumor, called an ependymoma, would still have to be removed, but because of the location, a much larger incision would have to be made on my wife's head to remove it; he cautioned that such an operation was risky because it was located in an area where she could lose such functions as speech, memory, or even worse, suffer permanent brain damage. We knew all too well that this could be the case, because a thirty-eight-year-old patient who was in a bed next to Tabitha had come back from having had the same surgery with the mental capacity of an eight-year-old. Dr. Cooper told us that the surgery would take about eight to ten hours if everything would go well. Like any other normal human being, I was very worried and concerned, but the Spirit of the Lord again came to visit me and I felt so strengthened that I told my father-in-law that I knew that everything was going to be all right. I give God praise because instead of eight to ten hours, the surgery was completed in less than seven hours, and she was able to retain all her mental capacity and functions. My God is an awesome God.

But God wasn't done yet, because after a few weeks of numerous follow-up doctors' visits and adjustment and calibration of the dosage of her medicine, and after numerous phone conversations, the time had come for us to settle up accounts with the hospital. I was directed to go see the cashier, where they would hand me a final statement of accounts. When they handed me the final bill, I could not believe the astronomical figure I was staring at and I thought, *How in the world will I ever be able to repay the thousands of dollars in medical bills?* Upon seeing the look on my face, the cashier advised me to go down to the financial aid department, where I might be able to get some help. When Tabitha and I got there, there was already a long line of people waiting to be processed. As we got closer to the front of the line, I noticed that the lady receiving the people was very loud and boisterous. She seemed to be flying off the handle at any little mistake that somebody might have done. Not that all people from New York are like that, but she sure seemed very determined in her Bronx-like mannerism to make life miserable for just about everybody. As we got closer, I was afraid that once she saw the slow reaction of Tabitha, she might actually go stark raving mad, but something funny and wonderful happened when we got to the window. She looked at me and then she looked at Tabitha and calmly asked us what she could do for us. As I handed her the application for financial aid and explained our situation to her, again she calmly made a couple of corrections on the application and then informed us that, unfortunately, we had missed the window of opportunity to qualify for aid, then she looked at Tabitha and gave her a reassuring twinkle and told us both not to worry about it because she was going to make the transaction retroactive so we could qualify. She then handed me back the statement with either a red or orange stamp on it and told me to take it back to the cashier and present it to them. After thanking her profusely and just as we were leaving, almost as though somebody had turned the switch back on, we could hear her ranting and raving again. The biggest part of this miracle was, when I handed the statement—now with that sticker affixed to it—to the cashier, she took it and thanked me. I then asked her what I needed to do next. Her response completely blew me away because she told me not to worry about it because the account was now paid in full. As I stood there with tears streaming down my face, all I could think of was again how awesome and wonderful and mighty my God truly was.

We knew that this was just the beginning of many challenges, including not only her recovery but also having to deal with her continuing epileptic seizures now, but after having seen the mighty hand of God in our lives in such a miraculous way, we were encouraged and strengthened to face whatever life might have for us because we were able to experience firsthand what Romans 8:28 declares: "And we know that all things work together for good to those who love God, to those who are the called according to His purpose."

CHAPTER 15

Show Me the Money

ONE OF THE challenges that we faced daily during the construction of the church was the continuous effort to try to secure the funds to keep it going. As I have mentioned in the past, most people just do not realize the tremendous amount of time and money it takes to even finish a corner of a wall. The skill that it takes to, first, lay down the cement foundation then to anchor the bottom wood beam, bring up the wood studs and the double wood studs, hammer in the wood spacers, drill through the crossbeams to secure the electrical wiring, put in the wall insulation, place the drywall and the tacking on the drywall then the first coat of plastering and taping, the second coat of plastering and sanding, and finally, the painting is only a small portion of the staggering detail involved in putting up any building. My respect and admiration for anybody who was in the construction industry definitely grew as I saw what it took to build our sanctuary.

We found ourselves, at different times, almost at the brink of having to stop because of the lack of funds. In fact, I once sat down and figured out that during the whole construction project, we had to come up with at least $1,000 per day. But as you will see in the next few chapters, God always came through for us. One day, we had reached such an impasse when the church treasurer informed us that we only had $9 in our construction account. We were already completely tapped out at the two hardware stores from where we had been getting our supplies on account. We really needed to come up with at least a few hundred dollars to be able to continue. I had gotten together with Mr. Alexander, and he had given me a list of the materials we would need to be able to continue. Because it had rained the night before, I had to take the time to clean off the mud from my boots as best as I could to be able to go look for some money. My strategy was to head over to one of the hardware stores to see if I could at least be able to get enough credit to cover the materials list that Mr. Alexander had given me, which totaled about $1,200. I was able to secure a little bit of additional credit, but unfortunately, it was nowhere near the amount I needed so we could continue working, so I drove back to the construction site with a heavy heart.

As I drove out of the hardware store parking, the Lord spoke to me in that familiar still small voice and told me to head over to Fordel, a fruit-and-vegetable packinghouse. I resisted the call from the Lord because the president of Fordel, Bob Johnson, had already contributed some money during the early phases of the construction project, so I felt that I really could not ask him for any more money at all. But the Lord kept tugging at my heart, and if there was one thing I had learned during this time, it was that I must obey the voice of the Lord. So I drove into the parking lot of Fordel, and I told the Lord that if it was really His will, to please help us get at least another $500 to keep going. I went into the office and told the receptionist who I was and asked if Bob Johnson would possibly have a few minutes to speak to me. When she checked with Bob, he told her to have me go to his office, but I informed her that I was wearing boots caked with mud. Bob still insisted that I come to his office, so there I was, walking to his office, apologizing to everybody that I was tracking mud on that beautiful, clean carpet. When I entered Bob's office, I could tell from the look on his face that he was more than a little annoyed. I looked at him and thanked him for the contributions he had already made and invited him to go and visit the project and have lunch with us. When I told him that the ladies would be serving some delicious Mexican food, his response was that he was on a strict diet, then he just kept looking at me. So I told him that he knew full well the reason for my visit. He curtly responded with a frown on his face and asked me, "How much do you need now?" I remembered that I had the list of materials that Mr. Alexander had given me in my pocket, so I handed it to Bob. He told me he would be coming by after lunch but made no promises. After leaving his office and after the frosty reception I had received from him, I began to wonder if I had done the right thing. This is where I've learned I have to trust the Lord because as he clearly states in Isaiah

55:8, "'For my thoughts are not your thoughts, nor are your ways my ways,' says the Lord."

Sure enough, Bob showed up about one o'clock in the afternoon, and he was pleasantly surprised and happy to see Mr. Alexander. They started to chat, and then Mr. Alexander took Bob around to show him the progress that had been made. Just as they took off, Bob turned to me and handed me an envelope. I did not know whether to follow them or not; instead, I decided to head over to the kitchen. I called the brothers and sisters that were working around me, and I told them to join me in a prayer that the check in that envelope would be at least $500 so we could keep working. After the prayer, I opened up the envelope, and in it I found that Bob had enclosed a check for $2,500. My God is an awesome God.

There was another time that as we got ready to make the final hookup for both the sewer and water lines, we ran into a big problem. While the water valve was right on the property, we could not find the main type for the sewer hookup. We knew that if we had to contract the city or some other company to find the sewer hookup, it could run into hundreds or maybe thousands of dollars to find it. Because we just did not have the money, we found ourselves again in a real dilemma. Later that day, as we got together, as we did every day, to have lunch, we had a visitor. As had been our policy from the very beginning, every day when we had our lunch together, anybody who has been invited or even who has just come off the street is more than welcome to come and break bread with us. This visitor had such a good time that as he sat there, looking full and satisfied and patting his stomach, he told us that he wished there was something he could do for us. Right then and there, I knew that the Lord had everything under control, for you see, this individual worked for the city of Mendota in the maintenance department. I asked him if he knew anything about how to locate and hook up our sewer line to the main sewer line. He just smiled and said he would be back the next day. Sure enough, he came back the next day and took out an instrument from the back of his truck that he would probably use to locate the connection we were looking for, and wouldn't you know it, the main sewer line hookup was indeed right in front of our building and, more importantly, inside our property. Truly, God was with us once again because He had turned a potential stumbling block into a stepping stone.

CHAPTER 16

The Secret Weapon

I HAVE NO idea how it got started, but once it did, there was no stopping it. It all began one day when it dawned on me that every time that God would give our church victory, we should do something to acknowledge His great feat. So one Sunday, after God had given us another victory, I asked the congregation to stand up, and I reminded them that like after every great performance, whether at a concert or a ball game or some type of special presentation, people would always show their appreciation by giving a standing ovation. I told them that from this Sunday on, with every victory that God would give us, we as a congregation would stand and give God a well-deserved standing ovation. I am not exaggerating to you that at that very moment, everybody (and I mean everybody) stood to his or her feet and started giving such a rousing applause that was so infectious and so powerful that it quickly turned into worship and praise unto God. You could feel that God was indeed pleased with this display of profound appreciation.

As you know in this life, along with victories, there will always be setbacks. If you will not have any setbacks, then you cannot really appreciate the victories that God will give you. Believe me when I tell you that during this time, there were many setbacks; in fact, many times, we found ourselves with our backs against the wall, and seemingly, we had nowhere to go. It was during one of the setbacks that God showed us that the standing ovations we were giving Him were actually a very powerful weapon, because if thanking Him for something that He has done is good, imagine what happens when you thank Him for something he is about to do. This principle worked quite well when we received a notice at the construction site that we were being assessed a $24,000 permit fee that all new construction projects had to pay for future school funding. We just did not have the money or any way to pay for this permit; as it was, we were just eking out enough money to keep the construction project going. But the hard reality was the fact that regardless of anything, the fee was due and payable now. We knew that the stakes were high, so we did the only thing we knew how to do; we went directly to God with this enormous challenge. That Sunday, I minced no words as I carefully explained to them the severity of our situation. I asked them how many thought that God was really with our church, because, I reminded them, in these types of situations, only by fasting and prayer would God be able to answer us. I told them that because we had been fasting and praying continuously for the last three years, I truly believed that if we believed on what God was about to do, we needed to stand up and give God, front and center, a standing ovation like we had never given Him before. The response was almost immediate and truly deafening, and with the worship and praise that followed, you would've thought that God had already answered our petition.

Well, the next day, as we worked at the construction site, always, as it seemed, in mud, somebody sent word that Mr. Singh, the superintendent of the Mendota Unified School District, wanted to speak with me. When I entered his office, I felt a little out of place because of the way I was dressed. Here I was in this fancy office, again, in my work clothes that, along with my boots, were caked with mud. It did not seem to bother Mr. Singh; in fact, he only seemed interested in one thing. You see, during that time, Mendota was in the midst of deciding whether or not to approve the construction of its first high school, and there seemed to be a lot of opposition to it. He wanted to know what my opinion was regarding this very controversial matter. Considering that at that time, our students from Mendota had to be bussed to another town to attend high school, I felt it was not only counterproductive but also dangerous for them to be bussed, especially during the fog season. I expressed this to Mr. Singh that I, in fact, was in favor of a new high school. He seemed not only pleased but also asked if I was willing to write an article in the paper in favor of it. I responded that I would be more than glad to do that. He thanked me, and then I turned around to leave. Then all of a sudden, right then and there, I felt a tug from the Holy Ghost to ask him about the pending $24,000 permit fee. He looked me straight in the eye and told me the following words: "Do not worry about it. It has already been taken care of." You can only imagine what the service was like in our next Sunday service when the church learned that God had come through yet again.

CHAPTER 17

The Lunch and the Miracles

I T SEEMED LIKE every day, more and more people went by to visit just to see with their own eyes this ongoing miracle, and as I had previously mentioned, anybody and everybody was invited, without exception, to come join us for lunch. When they did come, many were moved to either make a donation or to help in any way they could. We had a painter come and donate his time to paint both the outside and the inside of the church. There was also a carpet installer that came down and donated his time and his crew to install the carpeting. It seemed that the simple act of sharing our meals and breaking bread with whoever might come by turned into a tremendous blessing for our construction project.

What we did was every Sunday, during our worship service, we would pick up two offerings; the first one was to pick up our tithes and offerings, and the second one was called a lunch offering. We would ask one family to donate lunch for each day of the week, including Saturdays, and Sundays were always the Lord's day and rarely was any construction work done. We would ask that each family bring enough to feed the crew and anybody else that might come by because we would use the occasion of lunch also as an evangelistic tool. Our families were wonderful because they would spare no expense and bring fantastic homemade meals that would more than feed the whole crew, though once in a great while, when there was little money, we would take the crew to go have pizza. Of all the wonderful meals that were given, one of my favorite dishes was an enchilada dish made by Sister Graciela Marquez, because her enchiladas put the emphasis on the word *chili*! They were so delicious but so chili hot you couldn't serve them in a Styrofoam plate!

Another individual, who was a friend of Mr. Alexander, was so moved by what was happening that he donated a large storage trailer that we were able to use for storing all our materials, and to boot, the Lord gave us a brother who had just arrived, who had no place to live, who volunteered to stay on the property during the whole construction project. Again, God was responding to our needs in such wondrous and specific ways.

The fellowship and camaraderie that we experienced, where we would sit for lunch on that makeshift wooden table, were so priceless because not only would we break bread together but also, afterward, for a few minutes, we would discuss the Word of God, worship and praise God for what He was doing, and have some wonderful and memorable fellowship. It was a wonderful time because every day, no matter what the challenges were, God was always there for us, and as you will see, many great and memorable things, including miracles, happened at that large makeshift wooden kitchen table. Without diminishing the blessings and the magnitude of all the donations we had received, one of the most fantastic events was one that came to be because of a video camera.

Lunch with the construction crew.

RICHARD MEZA

CHAPTER 18

The Day the Roof Fell Over

O NCE THE WALLS were erected and the main beam was installed, we now faced the challenge of having to purchase and put on the roof. The roof—or trusses, as they are called—was going to cost us about $22,000, which, of course, we did not have. So we did the one thing that we knew we could do; in the next Sunday service, when I explained to the congregation that we needed the funds to purchase the trusses, we all stood up and thanked the Lord and gave him a standing ovation for what He was about to do. Sure enough, as had been happening, the Lord made a way by a donation that was given to us by Bob Johnson of Fordel of $25,000. God had come through again.

After taking the plans and the monies to the company that made the trusses, we continued working on the building as best as we could. As the day we knew the trusses would come in approached, we had to scramble to find somebody with a crane that could help us unload the trusses. It just so happened that Mr. Alexander had a friend who owned a wrecking yard right around the corner from the construction site; when we approached him about possibly renting his crane, he wouldn't hear any of it as far as renting the crane to us. He told me to let him know the moment that the trusses arrived and he would be more than glad to help out a neighbor by not only donating the use of his crane but also personally operating the crane. It was during these times when I would shake my head in amazement, look up to the sky, and thank God for His mighty hand in our lives.

On the day that we knew that the trusses were being delivered, we notified the police department because of the size of the trusses. I still remember standing on the corner of Ninth Street and Highway 180, waiting for the trusses to arrive, because aside from the police department, there were many people waiting for the semitrailer carrying the trusses to go through. When you consider the size and dimensions of the trusses, you will be able to understand that this was a really big event for the small town of Mendota. As the rig turned left from Highway 180 on to Ninth Street, I think the driver took the turn too fast, because when he tried to straighten out his truck, it fell over on its right side and spilled the trusses onto an empty parking lot. I could not believe what I had just seen. As I ran toward the truck, I feared the worst because if the trusses were really damaged, by the time they would send them back for repair, it would have put our construction schedule way behind. To my relief, when Mr. Alexander inspected the trusses, there was only minor damage, so with the help of our neighbor who used his crane to pick up the load and put it back on the truck, we were finally able to get the trusses to the construction site. I thank God that things did not turn out worse and that God continued to be with us.

It just seemed to be the case time after time, no matter what the obstacle might have been, that God was always on our side. Any of these incidents could have really set us back because as I have mentioned before, the worst thing that can happen to a construction project is a stoppage, whether it be because of money or some other circumstance.

Truck loaded with the trusses that fell over it's side

Trusses only slightly damaged despite truck accident.

CHAPTER 19

Joe and Liz and the Video Camera

JOE AND LIZ Neri have been our dear friends for so many years that we consider them more like family. We have known them since their son Abel came out on our wedding in 1977. We had the good fortune to have attended the same apostolic church in Escondido with the Neris up until 1986, when we left to go pastor Mendota. When they came to visit us in Mendota during the construction, Joe, who owns a landscaping business, felt in his heart that he needed to go help us install all the landscaping at the site. This was no easy task when you would consider that the trip from San Marcos (which is located in San Diego County) was more than a fourteen-hour round-trip, yet numerous of times, at their own expense, Joe and Liz would make the trip to go install all the piping, irrigation system, timer-control system, shrubs, trees, and sod. There is no way we can ever repay Joe and Liz for all the time and money they have graciously donated to the building of our sanctuary.

But Joe and Liz did not stop there, because they are instrumental due their friendship with others; these good folks also donated thousands of dollars in time and expertise for the construction of our sanctuary. Gus and Lupita Mikris (who own their own plumbing-installation company) would come all the way down from San Jose and donate their time and expertise to install all the interior hot- and cold-water plumbing and all the drainpipe system throughout our seven-thousand-square-foot sanctuary.

The most wonderful thing was when Liz came over one day and decided to make a video of the wonderful things that were happening in the building of our sanctuary and took it back to San Marcos to show everyone the great and mighty things God was doing in Mendota. The response was almost immediate, because I got a call from them that Steve Hernandez, a good friend of ours, was coming up with a crew of seventeen professional drywall hangers all the way from San Diego to help us hang more than five hundred sheets of five-eighth-inch drywall. Truly, the Lord was with us, for how can you explain such an awesome miracle? Even now, after so many years, I cannot help but rejoice in what the Lord has done for us so long ago; my cup runneth over because my God is an awesome God.

A couple of weeks later, this awesome group of volunteers went up to see us and immediately got down to business. The only thing they asked for was gasoline and lodging, and of course, after everything was done, we were only too glad to have given them a carne asada barbecue feast that we hoped they would never forget. The most amazing thing was to see how these consummate professionals worked in precise harmony—to see a man who weighed about 150 pounds (soaking wet) pick up a five-eighth-inch-thick four-by-twelve-foot drywall sheet, run with it, then hand it over to another man who was waiting on top of a catwalk, who then swung it up to a slanted ceiling that was almost fourteen feet up in the air, and then without hesitation, as he began to nail in the drywall, the first man joined him in completing the nailing of the drywall sheet. The most awesome thing was that they were able to hang all five-hundred-plus sheets of drywall in a little over twelve hours. My respect, as I have mentioned before, to all the people who work in construction, because as far as I'm concerned, you are worth the salary you are paid and more. Because of the video, we also received a generous donation for all the tape and mud (spackle) from another friend of the Neris, Eliseo Macias, which was needed to prepare the inside of the sanctuary in order to be able to paint it. This part of the construction (painting and prepping) was done by us, so if you happen to visit the church, please look the other way when you see the imperfections that we have left.

So many blessings, and all because of Joe and Liz Neri and their big heart and, of course, Liz's video camera. Thank you, Joe and Liz, for all that you have done for the church of Mendota. May God always richly bless you for your tremendous kindness and generosity for the work of the Lord.

Joe and Liz Neri

CHAPTER 20

The Bag of Oranges

IN MY OPINION, one of the biggest misconceptions about a construction project is that most of the expenses come at the start of the project because of the start-up costs, like the plans, permits, etc. What I have found out is that once the foundation is in and the walls are up and all the electrical, plumbing, drywall, texture coating, and inside and outside painting are completed, this is when the real expenses begin. We found ourselves in that very position because we now had to purchase necessary items—the carpeting and the pews—but as usual, money was a problem. We did what we had been doing any time a challenge arose; we went directly to God. As the church continued fasting and praying, and as we continued to give God a standing ovation every Sunday, we waited for God to answer. But as Sunday after Sunday came and went, it seemed like we were just not receiving an answer from God.

Just as we began to wonder if God would answer us, Sister Eva Salinas, our ladies' auxiliary president, called me and told me of a certain individual from another church that might just have money to loan us. When I heard his name, I knew exactly who she was talking about, because I had already had an encounter with him; it happened during a sector multichurch fellowship service about a year prior. A *sector* is a group of churches within a certain geographical area that is supervised by an elder, who is there to serve the pastors of the said churches. It was during this fellowship service in which this individual served as an usher when I and some other folks waited to go into the sanctuary through a side entrance. Just as I was about to enter, he decided to close the side entrance and directed everybody to go around and to go in through the front entrance instead. Because I was almost to the door, I asked him if it would be all right for me to go in since I was going to MC the service. He slammed the door in front of me and told me that I would have to go through the other door just like everybody else. People were shocked that he would treat me so rudely, since I was a pastor. But I understood that because I was a pastor, he was right and that I needed to set the example, so without saying a word, I turned around and went in through the front entrance.

Well, here we were a year later, and I thank God he remembered me when I got on the phone with him. He told me he would be glad to go down and meet with me at the construction site during lunch to see what could be done. The next day, after lunch, with my briefcase in hand, I stated my case to him. I told him what we needed and that it would cost around $10,000 or whatever amount he could possibly loan us. He looked at me then looked around at the construction site then looked back at me and proceeded to scold me because, he told me, the worst thing anybody could do was to go around carrying a briefcase because people would assume you had money in it. Just then, he reached into a brown paper bag he had brought with him and handed me an orange (that I thanked him for), then he reached back into the brown paper bag and handed me the last thing I would've never expected to see; he handed me a stack of brand-new $100 bills that, according to my mathematics, was the $10,000 we needed to be able to continue working. Think about this; he loaned our church, right then and there, without any collateral, just my word and signature—$10,000. Not only do I tell you that God is good and great and worthy to be praised, I also don't mind telling you that the orange that he gave me was also very delicious.

CHAPTER 21

Anything? and the Parking Lot

ANYTHING? IS THE actual name of a business in Mendota that fabricates (as the name states) just about anything you need. We had come to know the owner, Fred Serrano, because when we bought some new tires for the pickup truck our church used during the construction, he gave us a good price. He had already went over to visit us at the construction site a couple of times and, in fact, had already donated the use of a porta-potty he had set up for us, which he also serviced at no charge. This one day when he went over to join us for lunch, he turned to me and asked me if there was anything else that he could do for us. Well, wouldn't you know that once again, God was answering another pressing need that we had, and that was how to put in our parking lot. Many years before, when I was a kid, I witnessed something that really caught my attention; it was during the grand opening of a new shopping mall in El Centro, California, held during the month of August. For those of you who are not familiar with that part of the country, temperatures can rise to as high as 120 degrees Fahrenheit, and that was exactly what the temperature was on that day of the grand opening, which was unfortunate because the day before, the asphalt company forgot to add enough sealer to compensate for the high temperatures. It was a sight to behold when the tires of the cars in the parking lot began to pop and began to sink into the asphalt, and because of this, I was determined that even though the temperatures in Mendota were not as extreme, our church would be better off putting in a concrete parking lot. Sure enough, he was kind enough to help us put in the parking lot, including doing the surveying and the final finishing, all because our church was willing to break bread with others.

It was during this time that something very special happened when one morning, while we were using Mr. Alexander's skip loader to level out the area, the bulldozer broke down. This was especially critical in that the ground needed to be leveled out and watered down because the next day, the concrete would have to be poured for the parking lot. I can still remember that the men and I began to use shovels to continue leveling it out, then one by one, the women of our church (without even being asked to) also took up shovels and began helping us. Then without another word, more of the women and even some of the older children also began to help us; everybody, whether male or female, young or old, all just came together to finish the job. Forgive me for using such a controversial expression, but it was truly a magical time. By the time all the leveling, tamping, and watering of the sand was done, you could literally feel the presence of God at the construction site.

Another business that was a tremendous blessing to our church was Smitty's Towing. Smitty was the planning commission chairman during both times we applied for our conditional-use permits. He seemed genuinely moved by the heart and unity of our church, many times coming to visit the construction site, and he and his wonderful wife graciously made donations to the cause. God bless Bill "Smitty" Smith and his wife, Jackie Smith, and their family for all they have done to help make our beautiful sanctuary become a reality.

Men, women and children pitching in during
construction when the skip loader broke down

CHAPTER 22

It's a Boy! (Twice!)

THOSE ARE THE words that every father wants to hear— "It's a boy!" Though God has given me my beautiful Ashly Elizabeth (who will always be my little girl), the fact remains that little girls eventually grow up, get married, and take on their husband's name. So you can imagine my elation when my son Richie was born on May 19, 1989. As I held him in my arms, I could not help but thank God that He had given me a son that would carry on the Meza name.

For those of you that have been following us on our WordPress Release Memories blog posts on Sundays, you know that because of what happened to his mother when Richie was five months old, we did not have much time to enjoy our baby as much as we would have wanted to. This is where the following scripture comes into one's life, because it helps put into perspective that no matter what you may be going through, no matter how much things may go crazy, and no matter how your life may seem out of control, the fact remains that God is always in control:

> And we know that all things work together for good to them that love God, to them who are the called according to his purpose. (Rom. 8:28)

Tabitha and I had made up our minds from the very start of our marriage that we did not belong to us; rather, we belong to him. No matter where, when, and how, whatever His will was in our lives, we would always be at His beck and call. This is not some kind of romantic or emotional notion on our part; moreover, we're not doing this so we can be thought of as some kind of heroes, but rather, we both feel this way because we truly love God.

After God had given Tabitha and me my daughter, Ashly Elizabeth, and our son, Richie Jr., we thought we were complete. But much to our surprise (and delight), God had other plans for us, the birth of our second son, Isaiah Silvestre (his middle name after his grandfather Silvestre Pena). Isaiah was a special baby because he had to fight for his life right from the start. While he was still in his mother's womb, the doctor told us that there was a possibility that he might be born with a congenital condition called Down syndrome (formerly known as mongolism). He advised us that the only way to confirm this was to perform what he termed as an amniotic blood test, which involved them inserting a large needle directly into the womb to draw blood to determine whether he had Down syndrome (DS) or not. He told us the inherent risk was that the procedure could kill the baby, but at least it would give us the option to consider terminating the pregnancy if DS was present.

I am not here to judge anybody, nor do Tabitha and I want anybody to judge us, but after praying and having some frank discussions, we decided that instead of even risking terminating his life, we would rather have Isaiah born however the Lord would give him to us (even if it meant he would be a special-needs baby) and that we would be willing and we would be committed to love him and look after him for the rest of his life.

Isaiah was born (via C-section) at St. Agnes Hospital in Fresno, California, on December 2, 1991, at 12:33 p.m., an almost ten-pound bouncy and *healthy* baby boy. We took him home after a couple of days, and it seemed like everything was going to be all right.

Unfortunately, over the next couple of days, Isaiah kept running a persistently high fever to the point that one night, because his fever was so high, I made the decision to immediately drive him to Fresno (about an hour away) and take him straight into emergency at the Children's Hospital. Because of my wife's continuing seizures, I first secured her, then when I went outside to turn the car's engine on, I saw that the hood was slightly open. To my consternation, I realized that somebody had just stolen the battery of my car. With a sense of urgency, I was beginning to look for the phone number of the members when (unbeknownst to me that Tabitha had called her) Sister Eva Salinas (our ladies' auxiliary president) told me that her car was outside, ready for me to use to take my son while she assured she would look after Tabitha and my two other kids. Needless to say, we owe her a debt of gratitude for what she has done that night to help save the life of my seven-day-old Isaiah.

Once he was admitted and they ran a battery of test, they came back with the verdict that Isaiah either had viral or bacterial meningitis, and because of this, he would require hospitalization until it was determined which one he had and what the best treatment would be. As many parents would have done, I went to the chapel and got on my knees and cried out to God and asked Him for a miracle. This was when I truly understood the significance of the scripture in Jeremiah 33:3:

> Call to Me, and I will answer you, and show you great and
> mighty things, which you do not know.

I spent the next few days looking after Tabitha and my kids and tending to the business of our church (at this time, we were still raising funds to pay off construction materials debt), but every afternoon, I would head to the hospital to spend the night with my Isaiah. From the very beginning, we noticed that even at seven days of age, Isaiah had a certain grace about because he almost never cried and almost seemed to be happy and always smiling (especially with his eyes). I know this is hard to believe because he was only a few days old, but God knows that I am not making this up at all. Because of his age, they had to run his IV by attaching a small stent to the bottom of his foot, and would you believe that when they put it on him, he whimpered just a little bit (because of the pain). But as soon as it was on, he started smiling a famous smile, which included his beautiful big eyes. He was such a happy baby that I rarely got to change his diaper because the nurses would literally jockey among themselves to be the one to do his diaper change!

I remember that one afternoon, the Fresno University football team went to visit the children. Sure enough, Isaiah quickly became the center of attention to the point that the nurse in charge chided the football players to stop crowding around him and told them to fan out and visit the other newborns in the ward.

After seven days, the verdict was in; the doctor informed me that Isaiah had responded well to the treatment, and because it was the viral and not the more serious bacterial meningitis, he would be able to go home that very same afternoon. My God is a mighty God, and to Him be the honor and glory!

Isaiah is now twenty-three years old and has just been informed that he has been accepted to and will start attending San Diego State University beginning this fall.

Isaiah at 7 days old.

CHAPTER 23

Realization and Revelations

AS WE STARTED getting closer to completing the construction of our sanctuary, we realized that we now had two obstacles that were in our way—money (as always) and time. Yet these were the times that God would really show His power because time after time, somehow, someway, God seemed to always answer our needs. One day, when I got to the construction site, it seemed like nobody else was going to come to work there, so I set about the task of installing some outside chicken wire in preparation for the first coat (called a scratch coat) on the outside of the building. Because it was so cold and windy, I had a hard time putting up the sheets of chicken wire by myself, but somehow, I was finally able to put it on. To my surprise (and my frustration), I somehow put the chicken wire sheet upside down, so I just sat down and shook my head in disgust for the bonehead thing I had just done. I do not mind telling you that I was not only frustrated but also felt very discouraged because I was the only one there, and at that moment, I looked up to the sky (while wallowing in my own self-pity) and asked the Lord how He thought I was ever going to be able to finish it as I was just by myself. It was one of those moments when you feel a sense of futility and you wonder whether or not you have bitten off more than you can chew, but I want to remind you that it was not me but God who started this great miracle of the building of the sanctuary. To this day, I still shake my head in amazement and wonder how God was able to use this young and inexperienced pastor in the building of this church, just like in the case of Gideon when the Lord reduced an army of thirty-two thousand men down to three hundred so that no man could say that it was them but rather the hand of God that defeated the great army of the Assyrians. Sure enough, not even half an hour later, quite a few of the brethren showed up to not only help me put the chicken wire paper right side up but to also finish putting the wire paper around the whole building. This is what I call realization that God is always there for us no matter how bleak or dark the situation may seem.

Another time, as we were working outside on the entrance of the church, I was standing on a plank, finishing up some nailing of some boards, when I decided to step back to admire my work. Wouldn't you know that I fell straight down and landed square on my feet, but unfortunately, with my hammer in hand, I ended up chipping one of my teeth. As I stood there, nursing my chipped tooth, which hurt even more because it was so cold, the old adage that says "Pride comes before the fall" came to my mind. Then it happened to me again when I was working on one of the recessed lighting boxes in one of the classrooms. I stepped back again to admire my work and realized that a portion of the wood was out of whack. I stuck my hand in the box to hammer back into place the wayward piece. Wouldn't you know that I missed the piece of wood, and instead, I unceremoniously hit my thumb, which throbbed even more because of the cold. This time, I received the revelation that you can never be too cocky because those who exalt themselves shall be humbled.

The funniest revelation I had was when I was working up on the rafters about fourteen feet in the air, when I suddenly realized that I had fear of heights. I remember I fell onto my knees and held on for dear life. Then I heard somebody laughing, and I turned around to see that it was Mr. Alexander, who told me, "Hey, Preach, that's the first time I have ever seen you on your knees." I felt a sheepish grin come on as I got up and held on for dear life while I finished what I did. Another time, Mr. Alexander got so frustrated with me and my ineptness in doing construction that he turned to me and told me the following: "Preach, how about you stick to preaching and I'll stick to the construction because just like how I can't preach a lick, you just don't have it when it comes to construction." Every day during the construction and to this day, I thank God for the tremendous blessing that Mr. Alexander was in helping to build our church, and now that he has gone to heaven, I have no doubt that God has probably put him in charge of some heavenly construction project.

One other interesting thing was the fact that during this time, the Lord put in my heart that we should find a way to acquire a parsonage for the church because when we first arrived in Mendota, we found out very quickly that because Mendota is an agricultural town (especially during harvest time), housing was hard to find. So I approached the folks that were building the new housing by the church and asked them if somehow we could buy one of those homes. Lo and behold, God made a way for our church to be able to acquire a brand-new four-bedroom, two-car-garage home for about $62,000, which we were able to pay off when we got our final loan. The most beautiful thing is that the house is just right around the corner, within walking distance from the church. It just shows you how God never misses any details when it comes to something that is in His will.

Mr. Thurman Alexander

The author

CHAPTER 24

Getting Down to the Nitty-Gritty (Another Bag of Oranges)

AS WE BEGAN to wrap up the construction, as I had mentioned in the prior chapter, time became a real issue. I remember that once again, we ran out of money, and now we really needed about $15,000 to be able to tie up all the loose ends. But again, we hit a wall. Thanks to Mr. Alexander, we had been able to get many of the cosmetic items (doors, toilets, sinks, fans, three three-ton air-conditioning units, and various other items) on credit, but there were so many other things that were needed that we just had to figure how to come up with more money for. I got up that Sunday night and told the congregation that we really needed to call upon the Lord to intervene quickly because time was running out, so we all got up and gave the Lord the tremendous standing ovation with all our hearts all the praise we could muster. That very night, the Lord spoke to me and told me, "I want you to call the same individual that loaned you the $10,000 and ask him for another $15,000." I threw my hands up in the air and told the Lord, "There is no way I can do this because we already owe him so much money." But you have to understand that because I was so dependent on Him, God and I had an arrangement; He spoke, and I obeyed. So I called him and told him that the Lord (and yes, I blamed God) told me that I needed to call him and ask him for the additional $15,000. There was a long pause, then he told me that he would see me at the site the next day. Sure enough, the next day, he went by, and when I saw that he had brought again a bag of oranges, I knew that once again, God had come through for our church.

As the day of our inauguration came close, with all the arrangements and planning that had to be done, the pace to get things done began to become frantic. While there was an air of great anticipation, there was also a lot of tension because of the pressure to get all the last-minute details taken care of. This led to an unfortunate incident that was completely my fault. On the day before the inauguration, Mr. Alexander was really pressing me about how I was laying down some plants into the ground at the last minute; he was pressing me so much that I lost my composure and I snapped at him. He did not say one word; instead, he got up and got into his truck and left. I felt very bad because of what I had done, but because there were so many last-minute things to attend to, I soon put this incident out of my mind. Later that afternoon, Mr. Alexander went by in his car with his wife and called me over. He reminded me that because he had the last word regarding the approval of the permit of occupancy, if I thought that we were going to have the inauguration the next day, I was mistaken. He pointed out that there were so many things that still had to be done that it would be impossible to have everything ready in time. It was then that I realized that what was happening was a consequence of my actions earlier that day. I understood that I should have never lost my cool and acted the way that I did to the one individual who had completely given himself for over seven months to the construction of our sanctuary; furthermore, I truly understood that he had every right to be hurt. I remember that at that moment, I got on my knees and begged (and rightfully so) for his forgiveness. Upon seeing my sincere remorse, Mr. Alexander told me that he would approve the permit if by the next morning, everything was completely done. This is a lesson to be learned by all young pastors, that you always have to be vigilant and realize that any lapse of self-control can have dire consequences.

I gathered all the crew and told them of the challenge that we faced, and I asked them if they were up for the challenge, which most likely meant we would have to work through the night. Everybody told me that they were game to make it happen because of all that they had seen God do for our church, so we made a prayer, and then we all got down to business. Every little detail—from the ceiling fans, bathroom sink countertops, and separators to every electrical socket cover—no detail was left undone. Everybody, including those who had come by to visit us that evening, volunteered to help us complete this gargantuan task,

RICHARD MEZA

because we all had faith that God would help us, and as we all know, faith has to be accompanied by works. By the time the last screw was tightened and the last door lock was secured, virtually everyone had gone home and it was just I who stood there in amazement of what God had helped us as a congregation to accomplish, not only that day but also from the very beginning of this endeavor. As I walked out of the sanctuary, I realized that I only had one hour to shower and get ready before I would have to return for the inauguration. Even though I had not slept all night, my cup runneth over because of what God had done, and all I could say over and over in my mind was the fact that my God is an awesome God.

CHAPTER 25

Inauguration Day

O N APRIL 14, 1992, we began the festivities of our inauguration day by walking as a congregation from the old church to our new sanctuary. As we marched, we could not contain our deep joy and our profound appreciation to God for all the miracles and wonders He had done for this small but "giant in faith" congregation. We were supposed to have a police escort because our march was from one end of the town to the other, including having to cross a major highway, but for some reason, the police never showed up. But it made no difference to us because as we walked, we kept lifting up our hands and shouting praises to our God. Unbeknownst to me, the congregation had settled with wearing pink shirts and ties for the men and pink dresses for the ladies, and in fact, with my wife's help, I had also secured a pink shirt for me. We were honored and happy to have in attendance many dignitaries, including the president of our organization, Rev. Manuel Viscarra; our bishop; our elder; and many pastors, but the true guests of honor were all the good people who helped in the building of our sanctuary, most especially Mr. Thurman Alexander. As I had mentioned in the last chapter, the last time I had spoken to him was the day before, when I had inserted foot-and-mouth and had really upset him, but that morning, when he went in to do the final inspection, he seemed very pleased that we, with God's help, had met the challenge. But the most beautiful thing of all was when, during the service, we announced that, in appreciation for what he had done, the social hall would be named the Thurman Alexander Social Hall. He was overwhelmed with emotion and could not stop weeping.

During the service, we had many wonderful things happen, with people either singing or saying special words, then our president, Rev.

Manuel Viscarra, after preaching an inspiring message, proceeded to officially inaugurate the new temple. But the most awesome moment that happened that day was the individual who dismissed the service, for it was none other than the pastor who had told me that we would never build this sanctuary. He had been right when he said we would never build it because it was not us who built it; rather, it was built by the hand of our mighty God. We had over five hundred people in attendance for the inauguration, many of whom came just to see what God had done for this congregation. But the people that I consider the true heroes of all this on that special day were the small but spunky congregation of the Mendota Apostolic Church that dared to believe that God would move the mountains for them, and because of their determination and faith, that was exactly what God did.

After the service, we had a potluck and fellowship with so much food that people were able to have second and third servings. What made it special was the fact that the main dish was none other than our barbecue chicken. After a while, when everything was said and done, I began to feel the effects of not having slept all night, so I snuck off into my office, where I closed my eyes for a few minutes. But even as I rested my eyes and took a little nap, I felt so good to know that God had been with us from start to finish. By the time the activity was over and I had said my good-byes to everybody, I only had enough gas in my tank to go straight home, plop into my bed, and not wake up until the next morning in time for our first Sunday school in our new sanctuary.

The next day was very special for me because April 15, 1992, was my thirty-fifth birthday, and what a beautiful present God had given me. By the time the evening service was over and we all headed home, I wondered what the next few months were going to be like for our church, for you see, just because you finally are able to build a sanctuary, it doesn't mean that everything is over. I felt confident that no matter what challenges came our way, I knew that because of the spirit and determination of our church, we were going to be all right. In retrospect, as I think about it after so many years, I realize that I really had no idea that even greater challenges were ahead for our congregation and for my wife, Tabitha, and me and our children. These challenges were almost as daunting as the ones we had faced during the construction, but regardless, I thank God that just like in the case of our construction, He would also be there for us no matter how high the mountain of adversity came to be.

CHAPTER 26

Time to Pay the Piper

I'M SURE THAT we have heard many times that after winning a very important game, even the best sports team has to be careful not to have a letup for the next, upcoming game because of the fact that usually, during that very important game, the team usually expends all its energy, and many times, it finds that it does not have enough strength to win the next game. This is the way that we all felt; God had given us our sanctuary, so we felt we had won, but that wasn't the case because the game was not over yet. We spent the next few months paying the mortgage but also paying off thousands of dollars worth of equipment we had purchased by way of Mr. Alexander's accounts. Between all that was sold, we paid out about $7,000 a month until Mr. Alexander's accounts were paid in full.

In the middle of all this, my wife, Tabitha, began to experience a growing frequency in her seizures, which meant that I had to attend to her more and more. It was a challenging time, yet we still could feel the hand of God with us. Everybody stepped up to the plate and did everything he or she could to help contribute whether in time or money. I remember that on the days we would have our BBQ chicken sales, Brother Eugenio Salinas Sr. (who was a quiet and reserved man who said few words but spoke volumes with his actions) would be at the church at 4:00 a.m. to prep and light up the grill, then after doing all that, he would head out to take on a full day's work. Accompanying him was his wife, Sister Eva Salinas, who would make these out of this world-scrumptious "beans with chorizo." Then as the BBQ chicken plate orders would start to go out, thanks to Sister Mary Alice "Licha"

Lugo, who was our official BBQ chicken (is ready) taster and tester, no BBQ chicken plate would ever leave the premises without her approval!

Then the ladies' auxiliary group, under the direction of Sister Eva Salinas, who incidentally was responsible for those huge and incredibly delicious tamales, the church would churn out at least two hundred dozen of these tamales each time, tamales so big and good that we actually found out other people were trying to pass off the tamales they sold in the name of our church.

Still, the constant demands of having to generate the necessary funds were beginning to wear on everybody, and I do not mind telling you that it was beginning to zap my strength, and to complicate matters, it seemed like everybody was having a hard time finding employment. That along with the usual problems associated with any congregation began to take its toll on our church.

While we knew that God was with us, like anybody else who is in the midst of a battle, we began to suffer casualties. Some families in the church did not agree with how things were handled, so they decided to take matters into their own hands. They began by going house to house to express their dissatisfaction and began to affect others into also not wanting to go to the house of the Lord. I remember that I would go to the sanctuary and get on my knees and cry out to God and ask Him for wisdom on how to handle the situations. I really felt completely overwhelmed because of all these problems both of the church and in my home with Tabitha's health issues.

I tell you these things because from the very beginning, I have made it clear that when I wrote this story, I would present an honest portrayal of exactly what happened because it's very important, especially for young pastors, to understand that God is with you in both the good and the bad times. Furthermore, throughout all these experiences, I just never had a supernatural epiphany or even an angel that came and told me that everything was going to be all right. What I did have was my God that would guide me, encourage me, chastise me, and lead me every step of the way by speaking to me through that still small voice that I had already mentioned a few times. I had never felt an overwhelming confidence; in fact, most of the time, I found myself either worrying or fretting about these challenging situations, but every time, when it seemed like there was no way out and I would call out to the Lord, not once did He ever leave me alone. I stand in awe and with a profound sense of appreciation of how truly great and mighty the God that I serve is; to Him be the honor and the glory forevermore.

One other way that I had to pay the piper was with my personal health. Unfortunately, because of the construction, I began to develop (I am embarrassed to say) a bad case of hemorrhoids. Because we had been in the middle of the construction, I had gone to see a local doctor who put in a temporary fix; not only did the fix not work, but it also made things worse to the point that I was constantly bleeding and in pain. When I would go to church, I would always have to bring the small pillow to sit on because the pain was excruciating, and many times at night, the pain was so bad that I had to lie down on the wooden slat that was part of our sofa once the cushions were removed; even then, the pain was so bad that I would cry myself to sleep. One night, I received a call that one of the members was in intensive care in Fresno, which is an hour away from Mendota. As I got ready to go see her, I received another call that another member had just been taken to emergency in Madera, California, which is about another hour away. You cannot imagine the excruciating pain that I felt as I went to go see the first member in Fresno and the second member in Madera, and it turned out to be about a four-hour trip so that by the time I got home, I was beside myself with pain.

The pain was so bad that eventually, I had to leave with Tabitha and the kids to go with my family to Mexico to have surgery done. After a couple of weeks of painful recuperation, I was finally able to feel like myself again. I am not trying to be a hero, but if I had to do it all over again, I would not hesitate, because every step of the way—from Tabitha's sicknesses to my sickness to what happened to Isaiah at seven days of age—to everything else that happened during that time, we know that we were privileged to see the hand of God in our lives. There is no greater privilege than to see God move in your life the way that He did in ours.

All the events I just recounted left me so exhausted that I felt sometimes like throwing in the towel, but I knew I had the responsibility of seeing this project always through to its conclusion. I remember that I started to pray and fast and asked God to bring better days for my family and for the church, but that was not to be the case, for unbeknownst to me, even darker days were still ahead for us.

Half chickens being barbequed for the fundraiser.

Giant-sized tamales were a bestseller during the church fundraisers

CHAPTER 27

The Dark Days

THINGS SEEMED TO go from bad to worse because as hard as they tried, it seemed like nobody in the congregation could get steady employment, causing a sharp drop-off in tithes and offerings. It got to a point when I had to go seek out donations from other sources because though we had paid off our construction cost, we found ourselves struggling to make the mortgage payment. But I want to remind you about what I have said about the spirit and resiliency of the people of this congregation because in the midst of all of our troubles, our church continued to grow. Every Sunday service, we would stand up and continue to give God a standing ovation, and in every fundraising activity, we could count on the majority of the congregation. New families began to arrive, which began to have a positive impact on our church because of the revival that was present in each and every one of our worship services.

There was one occasion when we had to come up with at least $27,000 to pay some pending debts. I knew that because of our situation, this would seem to be one challenge that most likely would not be met. I remember that I called the church meeting to be held after our Sunday service. During the service, I hoped somehow, someway God would turn things around. The worship service turned out to be just a regular service, and though I preached my heart out, the altar call afterword was pretty normal, so I resigned myself to the fact that nothing short of a miracle was needed to help our situation. As I stood up to start the meeting, I took a deep breath and explained to them the challenge we had before us. When I was done, I just stood there, not sure of what was going to happen next. What happened next was totally unexpected because right after I spoke, a beautiful weeping spirit came over our congregation. It was something beautiful and magnificent to behold, and I had never seen this happen in all my years in ministry. One by one, people began to stand up and give what they felt in their hearts. How in the world this happened is beyond me, because as I have already mentioned, most people were either not working or disabled, yet somehow, they gave what they had. Some gave the savings they had set aside for a rainy day, and others, as a group, gave monies they had set aside for upcoming activities, like Pastors' Day. But the most beautiful thing was that once everything was over and after I thanked them, the dismissal prayer was so beautiful and so united that many of us could not leave because of how much the Spirit of the Lord was within our midst. After everybody left and I went back into the office to help with the offering, I wept even more because the total offering picked up that day came out to be $27,777.27! To God be the honor and glory, for my God is a mighty God.

In another occasion, at about 1:30 p.m., knowing that bank would close at 3:00 p.m., I found myself needing about $2,500 to be able to complete the mortgage payment with nowhere to go and no one to turn to to secure the monies. As I had done numerous times, I called upon the Lord and reminded Him that I had done everything in my power to do the works to back up my faith, that He would answer us, so I told God, "I'm going to sit here and wait for You to tell me what to do next." A moment later, the Lord told me in that still small voice to call Bob Johnson, who had already donated thousands of dollars to our church. When I called Bob, I told him that we needed to see if we could borrow $2,500. He stopped me dead in my tracks and told me it was not the policy of his company to loan money to churches. When I thanked him, he told me to stop by anyways to see if there was anything he could do. As soon as I walked into the office, the receptionist handed me an envelope and told me that Bob had told her to give it to me. After thanking her, I went outside and opened the envelope, and I saw that it was a check for the $2,500 I had asked for.

Unfortunately, because of our dire situation, the bottom finally dropped out, and we found ourselves five months behind our mortgage payments, which totaled a little over $17,000. I could use the excuse that if our organization had authorized the sale of our old property (which had a willing buyer), that would have immediately solved our dire situation. The bottom line is that as the pastor, the buck stops here with me, and I take full responsibility for the situation we found ourselves in. When I contacted our bishop and explained our situation to him, he assembled a meeting of all the churches and asked for help in the form of loans from them in order for us to bring our mortgage up-to-date, and I thank God that many churches responded and we were able to pay off the arrears. But it came at a very heavy price for me personally because my character and integrity were brought into question; many pastors wanted to know how in the world I had allowed this to happen, for which I had no answer. One pastor accused me of having reckless faith, others accused me of mismanaging funds, and others questioned whether or not I was competent to pastor the church. Though I was publicly humiliated, and though it really hurt me that many people whom I thought were my friends seemed to turn on me, I understood that I brought the situation upon ourselves, and in a sense, they had the right to question and to doubt and to judge. I also understood that I had to pay whatever price if I wanted to make sure that our church would get through this. The only saving grace was the fact that all these churches would be repaid once the sale of the old church property was approved and consummated. Again, I want to make sure for the record that I make no excuses for what has happened because I know that I bare full responsibility as the pastor of my church, but I do know that in my heart I have done the best that I can do to the best of my abilities, and that in itself gives me a small sense of satisfaction. This gave me strength during the next few months as I heard innuendo after innuendo from many different people, and though I went through what I went through, I thank God that I never lost my voice or my sense of integrity, because this whole project was never about me; instead, it was first about what a mighty and powerful God we serve then, secondly, about an amazing group of people who, through their courage and faith, was able to build a seven-thousand-square-foot sanctuary with virtually no money or resources in about seven months.

CHAPTER 28

In Conclusion

A S THINGS GOT back to normal and the attacks on my person and our church subsided, our church continued to experience growth and revival. While my children were doing well as far as their health was concerned, unfortunately, Tabitha's seizures began to grow in frequency and intensity. There were many occasions where when I was out tending to the business of the church I would get a call that she had to be transported by ambulance back to the hospital; furthermore, she had other complications like lapses of sentience where she had no idea where she was. I was becoming increasingly concerned because though we were thankful that we could take her to the county hospital, going to one of those hospitals can be a real challenge. For example, every time we went to an appointment, the young intern in charge would have to familiarize himself, right then and there, with my wife's (rather thick) medical file. I had to be on my toes to make sure she was not given the wrong medicine and/or dosage because this would have an adverse effect on her health. That along with follow-up visits to check on her progress that she recovered from her brain surgeries really put a heavy toll on my family.

Since I first got to Mendota, I had been getting calls from my former employer, who really wanted me to go back; he had been persistently calling me for the six years I had been gone. Seeing the steady progress that our church was making for the first time in many years, I stopped to consider that it might be time for me to go back home, not only because if I went back to work, I would now have good health insurance for my wife, but also because we had the support system of family and friends back home who could help me with Tabitha and my children.

It was really a tug of war in my heart because of how much I loved and cared for my church, but at the same time, I knew that as my family was growing and my wife's health was a priority, I had the responsibility to them as well. Then one Sunday night, we had a dear friend of mine come visit us to preach. When the service was over, I told Brother Carlos Ceniceros Jr. about our situation and asked him for his advice. Brother Ceniceros did not hesitate to tell me that he felt in his heart that it was time for me to make the move for the sake of my wife and my family.

So I confided in my assistant pastor, Brother Prospero Jacobo, and his wife and began to train and prepare them to eventually take over as pastors of the church, involving them in everything, from church administration to counseling, because I knew that the time was coming quickly to an end, when my time as pastor of our church would be over. I notified our bishop, then I had a meeting with the church where I gave them the news that because of the demands of my wife's delicate health and recovery from her brain tumor operations, I felt it was time for me to move on. It was a bittersweet moment for me as both Tabitha and I and the congregation wept, but I knew that I was leaving the church in the capable hands of the new pastors, Pastor Prospero and First Lady Esther Jacobo. We spent the next few days going from house to house, saying our good-byes and thanking each and every family personally for all they had done and for allowing us to have been the pastor for all these years. I still remember that after the service when I turned the congregation over to them, after the dismissal prayer, I felt completely lost. I did know whether to turn left or whether to turn right because for the first time in many years, I no longer had the responsibility (and privilege) of having this wonderful congregation to look after and to worry and care for. Unless you have been or are a pastor, you cannot understand the love that God puts in our hearts toward the congregation that He puts into our hands, because He expects us to love His sheep as much as He does, because He is the Good Shepherd.

We took the last $800 that we had received from public assistance, and along with the love offerings many good folks had given us, we loaded up the U-Haul truck with our belongings, said our final good-byes, and headed down Interstate 99 to our new home. As we went down the highway, I can tell you that I felt heartbroken because for six years, we had been privileged to have pastored such a wonderful and awesome people that to me could only be described as true heroes because of the heart and determination and love that they demonstrated during those years. As we drew closer to our destination and to our new home, we couldn't help but wonder what God had in store next for the Meza family.

CHAPTER 29

Epilogue

AFTER WE ARRIVED at our new home in Chula Vista, California, and I went back to work, we were finally able to get my wife the health care she deserved. Tabitha and I decided that we would take a small sabbatical from the pastoring because once we were home, we realized how truly exhausted we were. Pastoring in itself (as anybody who has pastored will tell you) is a very difficult and exhausting endeavor, but if you add the factor of a church construction project, by the time you are finished, you are totally and completely done. But then if you add everything that we went through, from the surgical removal of Tabitha's brain tumor and subsequent recuperation along with her continuous seizures, the meningitis scare of my son Isaiah as a seven-day-old infant, and my very painful (and very embarrassing) surgery and treatment for hemorrhoids, you cannot begin to imagine how truly profoundly exhausted we felt. I do not tell you these things to seek anybody's sympathy but rather, for those that have been in these types of experiences, I welcome your empathy. I don't mean to be redundant, but as I have previously said, we feel so honored because we have seen the hand of God in our lives.

Even after we arrived and for so many years after that, we continued to receive news about the church we so dearly love, some good and some news not so good. Pastor Jacobo, as I knew he would be, was more than up to the task, and after a few months of adjustment, the church was able to get back into stride. I definitely understood that once one leaves pastorship, there will be some that who will think you have done a good job and others that think you have done a terrible job, but as far as I'm concerned, the one judge that I pray thinks I have done an adequate job is the one whom I need to answer to, and that is my God. I say the following with all due respect because many of my fellow colleagues and those that I thought were my friends were the ones that formed a committee to investigate the books of the church, seemingly trying to find out if I had done something wrong. But as I had been taught by my pastor in Escondido, Pastor Frank Villa, I not only prepared a complete financial report, but I also kept a copy of it just in case any questions might arise. But even with the report in hand, these folks seemed determined to find that there was something amiss instead of considering that maybe it really was the powerful hand of God that had done this great miracle in Mendota. In particular, there was one pastor who, when I was building, kept asking me how in the world I was doing what I was doing even though many times I tried to explain to him that it was not me but the hand of God. Then when the financial crisis came, when we got behind on our mortgage payments, he became one of my principal detractors. For you young pastors, this is a lesson to be learned, that you realize that it is never about you but it should always be about God so that if your person or character is attacked, you do not take it personally but instead understand that it is part of the job as a pastor.

I can keep giving many more examples of how many times my person and my integrity has been attacked during the next few years, but it is important that you come to realize that you must always take the high road in the situations so that what has happened to me does not happen to you. Because I heard so many things, including rumors that I had bought my home with funds that I had absconded from the church before I left and also a ridiculous rumor that I had accepted funds from the Mexican drug cartel, I just wanted to set the record straight on just these two. The funds that we used for the down payment on our house came from the five years of appeals it took us to get Social Security to grant Tabitha permanent disability, and as far as the cartel story is concerned, we once were given the opportunity during one of the annual Mendota harvest festivals to receive a donation of $5,000; all we had to do was sign a document verifying that we were a nonprofit organization, but when we were told that it was for beer, out of principle, I refused to sign. What I did not realize was that because I was taking all these things personally, the spirit of bitterness took root in my heart. It affected me so much that for so many years, I was not able to write this book. It wasn't until Brother George Pantages (yes, the same individual who God used as a messenger at the beginning) spoke directly to me and rebuked me and told me until I repented and got rid of my bitterness, God would not bless me or the book that I needed to write when I realized what came over my heart, and right then and there, I repented and asked God's forgiveness. But the tragic thing is all the years that were lost because of my foolish bitterness. As I have already mentioned, there are so many other terrible things that were said, some ironically, during the time that my Tabitha got sick again, but I would rather concentrate on the fact that God allowed us so many great and wonderful experiences during those years, in Him.

So here I write this wonderful story about twenty-four years after it happened, during which time Tabitha had another brain tumor removal operation, had continuing epileptic seizures, had four major strokes, is now confined to a wheelchair for the third time (though she will tell you she is going to walk again!), had three surgeries because of TMJ (please Google it), and had been advised by her neurologist (who told Tabitha with tears in her eyes) that she is likely to die within the near future from either a series of small strokes or a brain hemorrhage because a razor-thin artery in her brain is fraying (and will probably disintegrate) because of the radiation treatments given to her after her last brain surgery. I hit an unfortunate peak of more than six hundred pounds (of which with God's help, I have lost almost three hundred pounds of), then I got borderline diabetes that almost cost me my left-hand index finger, which was saved by a grueling six weeks of every eight hours of double IV of antibiotics through a PICC line placed directly below my heart (I thank God I now no longer have diabetes); had knee surgery; and am about to have hip-replacement surgery. And yet we consider ourselves so privileged and blessed because as I have mentioned throughout this book, we have seen the mighty hand of God in our lives. Blessed be the name of the Lord.

Believe me when I tell you that there isn't a day that goes by that I don't question myself whether or not I could've done a better job because I know that I have made plenty of mistakes. This is part of human nature where we experience our would'ves and should'ves, but what's done is done; as far as I am concerned, what Tabitha and I have done (with all our heart), we have done it because we love God and feel this has been the best way we can demonstrate it to Him. We have been back to Mendota a few times, unfortunately, to go back to say our good-byes to some of the dear members that have passed (and some whose funerals we were not able to attend), good folks like Brother Santiago Madrigal, Brother Frank Gallardo, Brother Javier Gallardo, Pastor Severino Rangel (the founder of Mendota Apostolic Church), Brother Jesus Robles, Sister Maria Robles, Brother Ramon Rodriguez, Brother Eugenio Salinas Sr., Brother Jose Maria Molina, Sister Maria del Carmen Molina, Pastor and Sister Silvestre and Eva Pena (my in-laws; he was my prayer warrior who always had my back), and Sister Graciela Marquez. But the one that stands out the most was the funeral for Sister Graciela Marquez (who, as I had already mentioned, made the best and hottest enchiladas in the world) because it was there that God let us know that what we did in Mendota was okay. On that Friday night of her funeral service, I was privileged to preach the message and after, because of my condition, I sat down in the chair at the base of the altar. Tabitha and I were amazed and humbled that there was a long line of people that wanted to greet us. What was more amazing was that with our own eyes, we were meeting the third generation that now worshiped in this beautiful sanctuary. This experience in itself let us know that whatever sacrifices we had made and the small contribution that we made toward the building of this beautiful sanctuary had not been in vain.

After pastoring for almost thirty years, about two years ago we knew it was time for us to retire, and though we do not know what God has in the future for us, there is one thing we do know for sure (which has been the case during our thirty-eight years of marriage), and that is that we do not belong to ourselves; rather, we belong to our God. Amen.

ACKNOWLEDGEMENTS

W E WOULD LIKE to acknowledge and express our deepest appreciations for all those who have helped make the dream come true of building a new sanctuary for the Mendota Apostolic Church. The following are members of the congregation, some of whom were here before and some who came during and after the construction of the church. We also want to thank all those individuals and businesses to whom we owe a debt of gratitude for all the contributions they have made for this wonderful cause.

Mendota Congregation:

Francisco and Lupe Adame
Joel and Gloria Anaya
Matias and Teresa Barron
Paul and Mary Corchado
Juanita Cortez
Miguel Dela Cruz
Rene Duran
Rita Esparza
Celia Gamino
Gavino and Ernestina Gamino
Frank and Blanca Gallardo
Javier and Carlotta Gallardo
Elena Gonzalez
Mary J. Gonzalez
Dora Gutierrez
Roger and Patricia Hortado
Philip and Tabitha Gutierrez
Prospero and Esther Jacobo
Jose Leal
Bertha Lopez

Belizardo Lopez
Angelina Lozano
Artemio and Mary Alice "Licha" Lugo
Santiago and Elvira Madrigal
Arturo and Marisela Marquez
Clemente and Maricelda Marquez
Jose and Graciela Marquez
Jose and Carmen Molina
Juan and Rosemary Moreno
Consuelo Mungia
Ignacio and Estela Navarro
Rufino and Belen Ocañaz
Silvestre and Eva Pena
David and Donna Ponce
Benny and Liza Ponce
Severino Rangel
Jose and Carmen Reyes
Jose and Irma Rios
Martin Rios
Jesus and Maria Robles
Carmen Robles
Ruben and Sarah Robles
Sara Robles
Rocque Higuera
Leticia Rodriguez
Ramon and Estella Rodriguez
Joe and Tavita Rosales
Manuelita Salas
Eugenio and Eva Salinas
Armando and Carmen Topete
Manuel and Olga Topete
Adalberto and Maria Valenzuela
Paul and Maggie Velez
Danny and Isela Velez
Ricardo and Angela Zermenio

Individuals and Businesses:

Thurman and Jeanette Alexander
Alma Corchado
Ron Corliss (Mendota City manager)
Ernest Davidson
Wayne Dedmon (Fedco Co.)
Baudelio and Mary Gonzalez
Jerry Harris
Bob Johnson (Fordel Co.)
Tom Locke
Tony Lopez
Joe Lyons (architect)
Wayne Moles (Fedco Co.)
Little Joe Rodriguez
Fred Serrano
Bill and Jackie Smith (Smitty's Towing)
Alex Valdez

AFTERWORD

I PRAY THAT THIS book was an inspiration to your life; I am in the process of writing my second book which is tentatively entitled:

A Beautiful Work Called Bonita

It highlights the experiences that our family went through after we get back from Mendota, including further miracles from God that have helped us cope with many more health challenges (surgeries, strokes, financial, etc) as the Lord allowed us to establish a new work called Bonita, which became our labor of love.

CPSIA information can be obtained at www.ICGtesting.com
Printed in the USA
LVOW12s0949250116

471422LV00002B/151/P